Experiential Group Therapy Interventions with DBT

A 30-Day Program for Treating Addictions and Trauma

Allan J. Katz and
Mary Hickam Bellofatto

Routledge
Taylor & Francis Group

NEW YORK AND LONDON

First published 2019
by Routledge
711 Third Avenue, New York, NY 10017

and by Routledge
2 Park Square, Milton Park, Abingdon, Oxon, OX14 4RN

Routledge is an imprint of the Taylor & Francis Group, an informa business

© 2019 Taylor & Francis

Library of Congress Cataloging-in-Publication Data
Names: Katz, Allan J., author. | Bellofatto, Mary E., author.
Title: Experiential group therapy interventions with DBT : a 30-day program
    for treating addictions and trauma / Allan J. Katz, Mary E. Bellofatto.
Description: New York : Routledge, 2019. | Includes bibliographical references
    and index.
Identifiers: LCCN 2018008535 | ISBN 9780815395690 (hardcover : alk. paper) |
    ISBN 9780815395706 (pbk. : alk. paper) | ISBN 9781351183345 (e-book)
Subjects: MESH: Behavior Therapy—methods | Psychotherapy, Group—
    methods | Substance-Related Disorders—therapy | Psychological Trauma—
    therapy | Psychotherapy, Brief—methods
Classification: LCC RC489.B4 | NLM WM 425 | DDC 616.89/142—dc23
LC record available at https://lccn.loc.gov/2018008535

ISBN: 978-0-8153-9569-0 (hbk)
ISBN: 978-0-8153-9570-6 (pbk)
ISBN: 978-1-351-18334-5 (ebk)

Typeset in Baskerville
by Apex CoVantage, LLC

This book is dedicated to my wife, Esther
for her unconditional Love
and to my clients
who make every day a pleasure
and a challenge.

—Allan J. Katz

This book is dedicated to
Dr. Wilson Hickam
My brother, my mentor, a man of integrity, who has
touched my soul for God and the heart of Africa.

—Mary Bellofatto

Contents

Figures

Tables

Foreword
Turning Point Counseling & Consulting

January 15, 2018

In 2004 while in private practice I was searching for practical techniques to help my clients cope more effectively with their feelings and thoughts when I came across Dialectical Behavioral Therapy (DBT). I had always been a fan of Cognitive Behavioral Therapy (CBT) and had seen positive results for most part but not for everyone. Of course, as a therapist our challenge and task is to individualize our techniques to our clients. This continues to be my goal for my clients. DBT has provided another powerful tool for achieving this goals with my clients.

I frequently tell my patients that life is about the "F" word: Feelings. Those of us who have the skill set to manage feelings or emotions typically live a fairly balanced life. Those who do not, tend to struggle with their emotions often leading to dysfunction, anxiety, depression and sometimes more serious mental and physical issues.

Dialectical Behavioral Therapy (DBT) was developed by Dr. Marsha Linehan, PhD. I quickly found that DBT was the missing link for many of my clients. It provided two basic things which I felt the other therapies often lacked: structure and mindfulness. Structure in the form of the Diary Card with Skills Training and Mindfulness to target the specific thoughts and feelings.

Mindfulness is simply the ability to become aware of the present moment without judgment or attachment. Research has overwhelmingly shown that mindfulness is indeed a powerful concept in managing one's emotions and thoughts. Mindfulness was at the time missing in some of the other concepts and even in CBT. It has now been more effectively integrated at least in CBT.

However, the most powerful tool in DBT is the Skills Training and practice which is an integral part of DBT. Dr. Linehan provides the DBT therapists with powerful skills training in her *DBT Skills Training Manual, Second Edition*. This manual is an excellent resource for clinicians. Allan Katz, LPC, CSAT has masterfully designed a simple process for facilitating groups in his work, *Experiential Group Therapy Interventions with DBT: 30 Days of Exercises for Treating Addictions and Trauma* providing four elements: 1. specific group therapy interventions; 2. practical application of DBT skills; 3. an experiential format; 4. specifically related to trauma and addiction.

First, this work provides practical step by step group interventions for any therapist to teach and apply the DBT skills. Each topic is broken down into several steps including "Warmup, DBT Skill, Processing, Writing, Topic, Experiential exercise and Closing."

Second, each step is detailed to provide the therapist with what he or she needs to be successful in teaching and applying the DBT concept. This makes facilitation of group practical and simple.

Third, and perhaps the most exciting, is the Experiential exercise. In each session Mr. Katz provides the therapist with a clear and easily implemented experiential exercise to teach and further in enhance the learning and application of the DBT skill. Allan has extensive experience and training in experiential therapy. I have personally observed him utilizing experiential DBT concepts in groups with powerful results. This concept alone takes DBT to a new level as far as its effective implementation and application into the lives or our patients.

Lastly, Allan uses his extensive trauma and addiction training to provide clinician's with a practical application of DBT directly to the areas of trauma and addiction including the symptoms and issue that result from both.

I am excited about the practicality of *Experiential Group Therapy Interventions with DBT: 30 Days of Exercises for Treating Addictions and Trauma.* This work will no doubt provide clinicians with an effective and easy to use tool to guide clients out of their trauma and addiction and into true healing and recovery.

Bobby Scott, M.A. LM.F.T. C.A.A.D.C., M.A.C., DBT-C

Preface

Group therapists sporadically search for exercises, sometimes at the last minute, to fill up group time. This book is designed to be a therapist's helper. Whether you're doing warm-ups, teaching DBT skills, or group exercises, these proven experiential techniques will bring creativity and spontaneity to your groups or individual practice. These proven experiential exercises have been used successfully in treatment centers, group and individual therapy internationally to treat addictions and trauma, utilizing DBT skills as well as original educational topics. This workbook, in "cookbook" format, will contain concise plans for facilitating a group each day within a month's cycle. There is a theme for each day with a DBT skill, psycho-educational materials, experiential exercises, warm ups and closings. Addictions and trauma often go hand in hand and psychodrama and experiential techniques are one of the preferred methods for treatment along with DBT.

When you purchase this book, and utilize the creative exercises, you will liven up your groups and help your clients go deeper into their feelings while teaching them proven skills to regulate emotions, interpersonal effectiveness and tolerating stress in healthy ways.

Acknowledgments

In 2009, after a 30-year career as an entrepreneur, I started a hotline in my home to help Jewish people suffering from sex and love addiction in conjunction with an Israeli website, http://guardyoureyes.com. The hotline and subsequent phone groups I facilitated gave me a sense of accomplishment and purpose which I had never gained in my years as a marketing consultant and business owner. At the age of 58, I told my therapist about these feelings and she suggested I go back to school and become a counselor. I thought she was crazy! At 58, get a Master's Degree? That sounded ridiculous! Well, we discussed it further and I decided to go back to college at the University of Memphis to get my Master's Degree in Counseling. After two years of school and two years of working under supervision, I received my license as a counselor in the states of Tennessee and Mississippi. I still run the hotline as my pro bono contribution.

Traveling through my own journey of self improvement, I was introduced to experiential therapy at Onsite Workshops in Cumberland Furnace, Tennessee and said to myself, "I have to learn how to do this type work." But I was still an entrepreneur and had no inclination that I would make this a career choice many years later. Once I decided to become a counselor I attended many workshops on experiential therapy and psychodrama, at Experiential Healing Center in Memphis, Onsite Workshops near Nashville, Hudson Valley Psychodrama Institute in Highland, New York, and the Mid-South Center for Psychodrama and Sociometry in Tupelo, Mississippi. All of these trainings set the stage for leading trauma, DBT and process groups at an alcohol and drug treatment center in Southaven, Mississippi, outside my home in Memphis, Tennessee.

I am eternally grateful to my instructors and supervisors at Experiential Healing Center, Kent Fisher and Michelle Rappaport (see chapter 16 on SomEx®) as well as my co-author, Mary Bellofatto for her psychodrama trainings at Onsite Workshops and her contribution to this volume. I am also indebted to the trainings I received at Hudson Valley Psychodrama Center by Bill Coleman and Rebecca Walters, whose guidance has allowed me to facilitate groups effectively and professionally using many of the exercises in this workbook.

My internship as a counselor at Turning Point Recovery in Southaven, Mississippi paved the way for my training by Robert Scott in Dialectical Behavior Therapy. For the past five years I have facilitated groups with both teens and adults suffering from alcohol and drug abuse, self -injury, trauma, bipolar, personality disorders and suicidal ideation. I am a proud member of the DBT consultation group in Desoto County, Mississippi facilitated by Mr. Scott; and forever grateful for his supervision, counsel, teaching and support, always encouraging me to use my skills in teaching DBT experientially.

I would like to thank all my fellow employees at Addiction Campus of Mississippi's Turning Point Recovery for their support, love and encouragement over the past five years; where I've had the honor of honing my skills as an individual and group counselor. I would especially like to thank Esra Ahmed, my former clinical director, for her support in pushing me to be a more effective counselor and allowing me to teach other therapists many of these exercises.

Most of all, I would like to thank my clients, whose lives I have touched and in return given me a rare gift of appreciation for giving them a life worth living. I have learned many valuable lessons from my clients, who have helped me hone my craft and become a better counselor.

1 Introduction to Experiential Group Therapy Interventions with DBT

Poem: Bidding farewell

By Allan J. Katz

How can I let go
Of the places I've never been!
To the exotic lands I read of when young
The people, the scenery, the fantasies I dreamed of when
I was born, and a new world was unfolding.

How can I let go,
Of the places I went, but wasn't myself
Full of fear and trying to impress;
Busy living out expectations of others,
That nothing real was really occurring.

How can I let go,
Of the people I never did meet?
People I admired and longed for their friendship.
Kept away by fantasy, fears and unworthiness,
So I could never reach my potential.

How can I let go
Of those I did meet but wouldn't let in?
So sure they wouldn't see the real me,
So fearful of what they would say, think or do
That I kept all conversation to a minimum.

How can I let go
Of my potential that was never used?
The hero, the scapegoat, the
lost child, the chief.
Yes, beggar and shyster, the clown and thief
Locked in my basement by fear or by grief.

Hole in the Soul

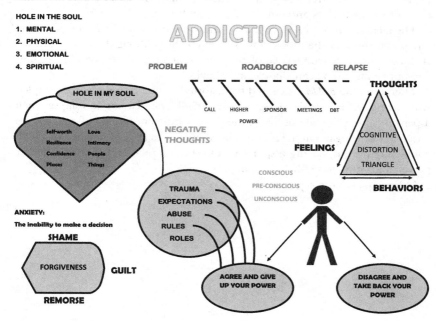

Figure 1.1 Hole in the Soul

To the group leader: The above illustration is a lesson in itself. It encompasses the multiple layers of loss experienced with trauma, expectations, neglect, or abuse. The hole in the soul concept has four parts: Mental, physical, emotional, and spiritual, each with its own unique twist of the psyche causing shame, guilt, and distorted thinking. In the illustration, the positive elements to fill up the hole in the soul are shown in the red heart. When a person has negative thoughts, they can be traced back to trauma, expectations, abuse, rules, and roles, shown in the blue circle. What were the rules in the household that created a void? What was the role the client played in relationship to their family? These potentially traumatic negative thoughts can be conscious, pre-conscious or unconscious, each delivering a blow to self-esteem; leading a person to fill the hole in the soul with addictive substances, food, sex, gambling, shopping, video games, etc.

When a person agrees that he must reach unrealistic expectations set by others and the rules and roles shape his behavior and feelings about himself, he gives up his power to trauma and abuse. His life is hindered by perfectionism and procrastination and he lives recreating his past or worries about the future, placing his well-being in the hands and expectations of others. However, when he disagrees with the rules and roles he was taught and begins to set rational expectations of himself, while working to minimize the effects of trauma and abuse, he takes back his power. These negative emotions and unrealistic expectations cause guilt, shame, and remorse, caused by self or others until they can forgive themselves and others for the past trauma.

The illustration continues with the cognitive distortion triangle beginning at any point, showing the interaction between feelings, thoughts, and behaviors. It shows when a person lets go of negative thoughts and observes his feelings without acting out he can change his behavior.

Therefore, the *problem* is caused by distorted thoughts and feelings coupled with acting out behaviors. These present roadblocks leading to relapse when a person cannot or will not live in the present moment instead of reliving the past and worrying about the future. The solution is to use DBT skills along with contacting friends, having a sponsor, cultivating a relationship with a higher power, and going to self-help meetings.

Otherwise, relapse is possible.

DBT Skill: Act Dialectically

The word dialectic comes from the Greek word *dialectic*, which takes the position that two seemingly opposite ideas can co-exist, without diminishing one another. For example, it is possible to want to be sober and to still want to abuse substances. It is possible to love someone and be mad at them at the same time. It is possible to be happy about one part of your life and sad about another.

For the addict or trauma survivor, acting dialectically helps you get rid of black and white thinking, good or bad, right or wrong, perfect or imperfect while considering the gray area may be a more sensible choice to balance your life. We accept the fact that people may not believe what we believe, may not act like we think they should act, and begin to practice a more middle path, balanced approach to life, feelings, and relationships.

When you are experiencing a craving, you can use the dialectic to help you understand you may not end up using when you make the decision to surf your feelings like a wave in the ocean instead of acting on every impulse. Many addicts believe they need to act out when they experience a negative feeling. By using the dialectic, you simply ride the wave of the emotion, as it rises and increases in strength and then falls, all in a few moments.

Theme: The Relationship between Trauma, Addiction, and DBT

There is a mysterious connection between trauma and addiction. Addiction can be caused by many factors including genetics, emotional abandonment or neglect, or growing up in a very strict household where you feel you don't have a voice to express feelings. For a small child, growing up not being able to express feelings or not having your feelings validated and comforted can be a traumatic experience. When trauma strikes, children utilize three options: Fight, flight, or freeze. Some children act out in school, others run away, and some freeze by going to their room and tuning out of reality into fantasy. Any response to trauma becomes a fertile field for addiction.

"Drugs and alcohol, for the trauma survivor, can provide a way to quiet the mind and body which they can have control over; a sort of self-administered medication" (Dayton 2011). Triggers occur when the addict re-experiences the shaming thoughts he thinks about himself from past trauma and uses alcohol and drugs to protect him from further emotional harm. He doesn't have to think about the emotional pain when he is drunk or high: "The more these substances or behaviors are used to quiet and calm unwanted feelings and sensations, the more dependent we become on them and the more convinced we become that we cannot calm down or feel ok without them" (Dayton 2011).

Dialectical Behavior Therapy (DBT) is all about training the mind to lessen emotional suffering. On one hand, DBT believes a person is doing the best he can do given his circumstances and he is accepted unconditionally. On the other hand, there is always room for change and growth. With consistent practice of the DBT skills, we learn to relate to our emotions and struggles in a different, more healthy way, learning to cope with life's ups and downs that will inevitably occur.

DBT does not focus on right vs. wrong, good vs. bad, weak vs. strong. Instead, it's about creating a life worth living, focusing on the results we want out of life. We practice being non-judgmental of others and learn to radically accept our past, ourselves and others, realizing we cannot change the past or predict the future.

According to Marsha Linehan (1993), developer of DBT, numerous scientific studies have found that DBT is effective in helping people manage their emotions, and decrease problem behaviors including substance abuse, suicide attempts, self-harm, and eating disorders. Linehan hypothesized (Koerner, 2012) that three factors contribute to a person's vulnerability. First, people prone to emotion dysregulation react with high sensitivity. Second, they experience and express emotions intensely. Third, they experience a longlasting arousal that is more difficult to tolerate.

People suffering from trauma and addiction are more prone to experiencing these fluctuating levels of emotions. People with addiction tend to abuse substances when they experience any form of negative emotion. Some use a positive feeling of euphoria or good news as a rationalization for continuing their substance use. Trauma survivors experience a heightened level of emotional dysregulation including startle response, trauma bonding, and trauma repetition. DBT skills help a person regulate emotions, tolerate stress, live a more balanced life, and reach her goals through more effective interpersonal relationships.

Life will be more meaningful when you identify the character traits you want to change, how willing you are to change your emotional state, and what you want most out of life (dreams, goals, values, family, career, etc.).

Act Dialectically Experientially

Note to group leader: A spectogram is a linear imaginary line drawn on the floor from one end of the room to another. One side represents zero and one side represents 100. Or you can substitute numbers for "very much" and "very little" or any other combination of extremes.

In this floor exercise, set up one side as "very much" and the other as "very little."

VERY MUCH---VERY LITTLE

Have group members stand at any point on the spectrum as you give them each one of these scenarios:

I am committed to change
VERY MUCH---VERY LITTLE
I believe in recovery
VERY MUCH---VERY LITTLE
I have what it takes to lead a better life
VERY MUCH---VERY LITTLE
I meet other people's expectations
VERY MUCH---VERY LITTLE
I am accepting of differing opinions and beliefs
VERY MUCH---VERY LITTLE
I think in terms of situations being either black or white
VERY MUCH---VERY LITTLE

Ask each group member as they stand along the line why they are standing in that position. This engenders more group cohesion in understand differing viewpoints and beliefs.

Closing: Commitment to Change/
Angle of Opportunity

This structured psychodrama exercise was developed by Bill Coleman, MSW, TEP.

Each of Bill Coleman's exercises are newly updated with additional material and can be found in the full-length book, *The Illustrated Guide to Psychodrama*, copyrighted, imprint 2017, to be published in 2018. For further information, please visit www.cwcolemanbooks.com and/or contact him by email at coleman151@mac.com.

It can be used as an introduction to DBT by exploring a choice they have to make and a commitment to change. It is also a means of future projection, giving the client an opportunity to plan, dream, and prepare for a future without drugs and alcohol. This exercise is about *behavior*, not feelings or states of mind such as depression and anxiety. The purpose is to help the client explore the differences between living a future with substance abuse vs. a sober life without destructive behaviors.

Setting the Stage by Facilitator

If I could teach you a few tricks about how to not be so emotional, who would be interested in knowing? How do you deal with challenges in your life? What are the feelings associated with these challenges? Anxiety, anger, fear? What do you do when you get that way? Would you like to know a better way of dealing with those emotions? How does attitude protect you? Thank God you've got an attitude!

Set Up

Set up three chairs at an angle on the right side and three chairs on the left side in a "v" shape. Each chair represents a period of time, say 3 months, 1 year, 3 years. For addiction, you might want to use 30 days, 90 days, and 1 year.

Finding the person who has a choice

Who wants to explore a choice you have to make? Let's look at the choice to self-harm (cutting) or not.

Action

The client sits in the 3-month chair and moves to the other chairs as the action continues. In the first scenario, we are going to explore what will happen when the client continues cutting and self-harming:

• You've continued to cut for 3 months. Where are you? How do you feel? What is the relationship with your family? Have they seen the cuts? What does your mother say? Are you working? Do you have a boyfriend (or spouse)? How does he feel about your cutting?

- Now it's 1 year and you're still cutting. Where are you? What type of clothes are you wearing? Are you working? Are you in school? What is the relationship with your family? Have they seen the cuts? What does your mother say? Are you working? Do you have a boyfriend (or spouse)? How does he feel about your cutting?
- You're now __ years old. OMG, you're so old and still cutting? Where are you living? With who? Do you have a job? Are you married? How does your husband deal with it? What does he say?
- Group: What do you think?
- Now have the client go back to the 3-month chair and go the opposite way toward not cutting.
- You have not cut for 3 months. How did you do that? What's one thing that helped you accomplish this? Who's one person that helped you? What do you do when you feel tempted to cut? How has not cutting helped you?
- Now it's 1 year and you have still not self-harmed. Are there situations where you wanted to cut but didn't? How did you do it?
- Now it's 3 years and you still haven't cut yourself. What are some moments you felt like cutting but didn't since year 1?
- Have the client turn back to the beginning and look at her younger self. What advice would you give her looking back?
- Group: What do you think?

2   Big T and Little t Trauma

Warm Up: Experiencing Trauma's Symptoms

Note to group leader: A spectogram is a linear imaginary line drawn on the floor from one end of the room to another. One side represents zero and one side represents 100. Or you can substitute numbers for "very much" and "very little" or any other combination of extremes.

In this floor exercise, set up one side as "very much" and the other as "very little."

VERY MUCH---VERY LITTLE

Have group members stand at any point on the spectrum as you give them each one of these scenarios:

I play by the rules
VERY MUCH---VERY LITTLE
I have a problem self-regulating
VERY MUCH---VERY LITTLE
I am easily triggered
VERY MUCH---VERY LITTLE
My relationships are healthy
VERY MUCH---VERY LITTLE
I have unresolved grief
VERY MUCH---VERY LITTLE
I engage in high risk behaviors
VERY MUCH---VERY LITTLE

Ask each group member as they stand along the line why they are standing in that position. This engenders more group cohesion in understand differing viewpoints and beliefs.

DBT Skill: Effectiveness

Effectiveness is a DBT core mindfulness skill and is all about doing what works, playing by the rules, letting go of vengeance, anger, and who is right or wrong. It comfortably accents the idea of recognizing the polka dots of life, opportunities for growth without judgment, giving people the benefit of the doubt, and not holding on to old resentments, jealousy, and revenge.

To be effective in life, you have to know what your goals are. Not having a goal in life is like walking in a forest without a map. You have no idea where you're going, how to reach your destination, and how to get out of danger. When a person has a goal, he has something to look forward to achieving and this becomes the impetus to move forward, despite the odds, to accomplish something in life.

When you accept a situation, you are being more effective. People are naturally more effective when they stop saying things should be this way or that way. It means playing by the rules even when you don't think they are fair. Without rules, our lives would be chaotic. Playing by the rules helps bring order and mindfulness into our lives, so we can accomplish our goals and be as effective as possible.

Being effective also means letting go of trying to get even with someone who has hurt you. It is a natural reaction to want to get even but hardly effective in creating a meaningful relationship. Instead, learn to give people the benefit of the doubt; try to understand the situation from their point of view. If your anger is justified, express it without rage. Or, let go of the anger of who is right or wrong and focus on an effective solution. Many times our anger is not justified and we let what others are doing or saying disturb our peace of mind. Being effective is letting go of extremes and focusing on the compromise position or mutual benefit.

Theme: Big T and Little t trauma Long Term Deprivation – Peter Levine

Trauma is stored in the survival part of the brain, so Talk Therapy, which is more logical, is not as effective as experiential methods to heal from its effects. One of our goals is to help clients modulate between body sensations and thoughts, feelings and experiences to reach a point of calm, even when feelings become overwhelming.

There are two types of trauma. Big *T* trauma and little *t* trauma. Big T trauma consist of infrequent or one-time events that are catastrophic, such as floods, earthquakes, hurricanes, 9/11, rape, and bone-crushing car accidents. Little t trauma is subtler, occurring over and over again during a certain period of time, even years. Little t trauma includes emotional or physical abandonment, growing up without a "voice," and being constantly yelled at, with strict, autocratic rules.

These insecure attachments cause a small child to fight, flight, or freeze. They begin to act up in school, run away, or simply isolate, fantasizing and playing to escape the pain. They become closed off to the rest of the family, living in their own little world of make believe, dissociating from their emotions, becoming passive, withdrawn, and lethargic. Little t trauma can be more devastating to the adult than big T trauma because it occurs over a longer period of time and is more subtle.

According to Tian Dayton, PhD, "psychodrama and sociometry allow the client to directly engage with the experiences on a visceral level. Before they are asked to talk "about" their stories, they have the opportunity to allow the many components of their experience to emerge naturally. Gradually, their thinking mind can move past its frozenness and come back on line and witness the self in action. This strengthens the observing ego and promotes emotional regulation through action insight and understanding. All of this happens in a group context, the group challenges, supports, witnesses and provides a container to help "hold this powerful process."

Adaptation of the Trauma Egg

RULES   TRAUMA EGG   **ROLES**

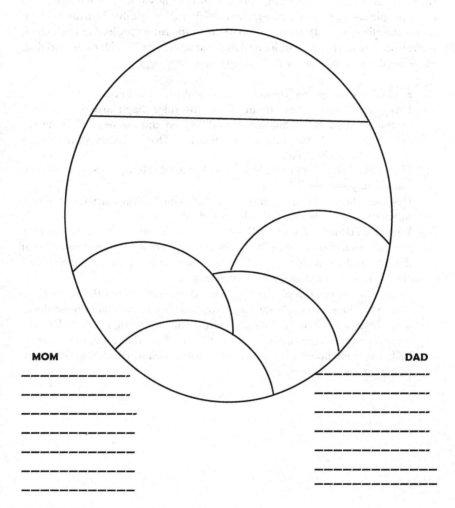

MOM   **DAD**

Figure 2.1 The Trauma Egg

Directing the Trauma Egg

The trauma egg is an experiential exercise that forms the basis for treating your client's trauma. The shame and sometimes survivor's guilt causes the client to shut down and not talk about her feelings. This is counterintuitive because the way to heal shame is by talking about it and being vulnerable enough to let other people know. The trauma egg, first developed by Marilyn Murray in 1983, allows the client to see the connection between the rules they learned as a child, the role they played in the family, and the characteristics of both mom and dad. Here are the instructions for facilitating the trauma egg:

1. Explain the difference between big T and little t trauma.
2. Using the diagram, have them fill out the rules they learned as a child. Examples might be: "Children should be seen and not heard," Don't cry or I'll give you something to cry about," "Don't discuss your father's drinking in public," etc.
3. Have them fill out the family role they played: Hero, scapegoat, addict, lost child, jester, etc.
4. Describe characteristics of mom and dad: Hard worker, strict, depressed, successful, alcoholic, emotionally unavailable, etc.
5. With a marker, have them DRAW a picture in the cracks of the egg, of each traumatic experience from birth at the bottom until this moment at the top. Tell them this is for them and they do not have to share if they choose not to, although we do encourage it.
6. At the line at the top of the egg, have them write down the *moral of the story*. After looking over what they wrote and drew, have them write down three irrational, shameful thoughts they still say to themselves. Explain that when these same thoughts enter the mind in adulthood, people react by filling their hole in the soul with alcohol, drugs, gambling, sex, food, shopping, video games, etc.

The Original Trauma Egg

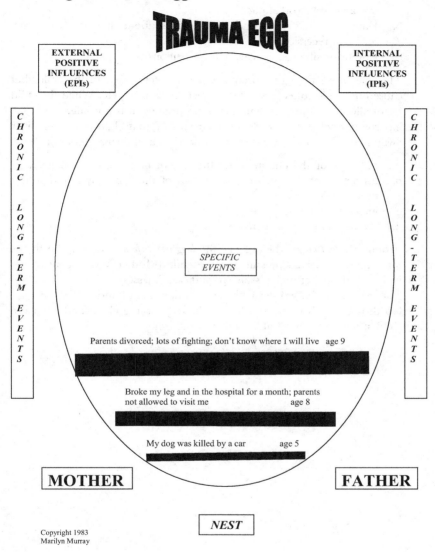

Copyright 1983
Marilyn Murray

Figure 2.2 The Original Trauma Egg

1. The egg represents the original child.
2. The bottom of the page represents the "nest" into which the child was born. List the following:

    a. "Mother" and "Father" and items about them that related to what affected their life at the time of the child's birth. (Oldest of

10 children, his father a violent alcoholic, age 6 when mother died, overachiever, workaholic.)

b.   Date of child's birth and any specifics about that era (war time, financial recession, etc.).

c.   Any prior siblings, miscarriages, or stillbirths.

3.   The lines *inside* the egg represent *events* that happened to the child that caused the child to feel pain, fear, rejection, sadness, etc. When the child is not allowed to process that pain appropriately (it is not safe, or no one has role modeled how to do so) then part of that child begins to sliver away and the sobbing child starts to develop and forms a pool of pain:

a.   the *width* of the line indicates the *intensity* of the traumatic event

b.   list on top of the line the *event* and *age* of the child (my grandmother dies, age 5)

c.   include present day events

d.   use as many sheets as necessary.

4.   Around the *outside* of the egg, list the *long-term, chronic stressors*, the things that created external pressure on the child (Mother – very controlling; Father – alcoholic; racial issues/prejudices; illnesses).

5.   The events can be written with the non-dominant hand.

6.   Go through each event and list the feelings of the child (and what the child should have been able to feel at the time).

Closing: Introduction to Psychodrama:
Telling the Trauma Story

> Our lives are reflected by the experiences of our past. They are always with us,
> inside ourselves, looking out.
>
> Allan J. Katz

Psychodrama is a clinical method of experiential psychotherapy that uses action
methods and the expressive arts useful in the healing of trauma. Psychodrama
is referred to as the four ABCs: Affect, Behavior, Cognition, and Spirituality.
The developmental roles of psychodrama consist of the double, mirror and role
reversal so that the individual can experience the inner self, and look at oneself
through the lens of another.

This exercise allows a client to tell a short story (2–3 minutes) about a painful
time, event, or place of confusion that they keep returning to in their mind.

Set Up

Place three chairs side by side with the following signs:

Chair 1: Facts
Chair 2: Feelings
Chair 3: Values and Beliefs
Chair 4: Protagonist sits and faces the three chairs

Directions

This is a group exercise where the protagonist (client doing the "work"), shares
a story 2–3 minutes' long to three people who have volunteered or were chosen
by the director of the group. The protagonist shares their story, each auxiliary
sitting in the chairs repeats what they heard, starting with facts, then feelings,
then values and beliefs. The audience is then asked to come and stand behind the
chairs if they heard anything different that has not been shared from the three
chairs. When finished, ask the protagonist what it was like to hear their story
doubled (played back by auxiliaries) and allow the three auxiliaries to share how
they connected to the protagonist's story. If time permits, allow the entire group
to share. This process allows the protagonist to hear his story through different
filters, and often allows him to find a deeper part of himself, to become aware
of his internal process, or find alternative ways of coping.

Looking Back

Set up two chairs facing each other and have each client select another group
member to play the part of someone who caused them trauma: Parent, relative,
perpetrator, sibling, other. Have the client go back in time and assume the role
of the child talking to one of these people, keeping in mind the perpetrator may

have changed by now, not to negate any positive current feelings. Be careful how you deal with the perpetrator, make sure the client has a strong ego and is prepared to do this work.

Writing a Letter

Have the client write a letter to the abuser or perpetrator. Experiential letter writing's purpose is to allow feelings to flow out of the body and onto paper. They are meant for contemplation, not to be sent to anyone. Letter varieties can include the following:

- Taking stock of where the client is now
- How has client been affected as a child and as an adult
- A letter correcting the false responsibility for the trauma
- A letter to the addiction or disease
- A letter from the adult telling the inner child what she wished she had for support when she was going through the trauma

3 Grief, Loss, and Mourning

Warm Up: Mind Benders

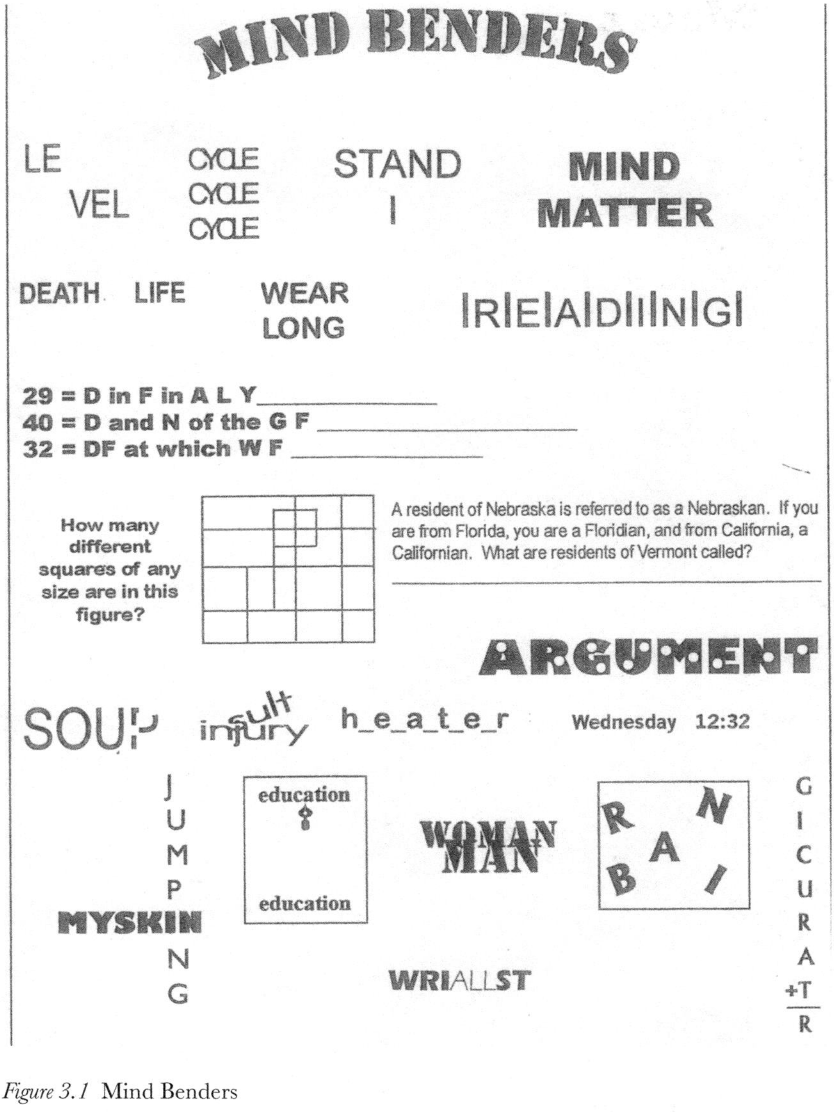

MIND BENDERS

LE   CYCLE   STAND   **MIND**
  VEL   CYCLE   I   **MATTER**
       CYCLE

DEATH. LIFE   WEAR |R|E|A|D|I|N|G|
          LONG

29 = D in F in A L Y_____
40 = D and N of the G F _____
32 = DF at which W F _____

How many different squares of any size are in this figure?

A resident of Nebraska is referred to as a Nebraskan. If you are from Florida, you are a Floridian, and from California, a Californian. What are residents of Vermont called?
_____

ARGUMENT

SOU$^{|}$P   in$^{cult}_{jury}$ h_e_a_t_e_r   Wednesday 12:32

J
U
M
P
MYSKIN   P
N
G

education
♀
education

WOMAN
MAN

R   N
  A
B   I

WRIALLST

G
I
C
U
R
A
+T
—
R

Figure 3.1 Mind Benders

Theme: Getting the Self Back: Grief, Loss, and Mourning: Moving Through Loss

Numbness: Respect this stage, regain connection to self through blocked emotions

Yearning and searching: Words not spoken can be spoken

Disorganization, anger, despair: Allow anger to rise to the surface, here and now

Reorganization, integration: Reintegrate the loss into the self, leading to new awareness

Reinvestment: Learn to relate to people differently

To the facilitator: Using the floor sheets in Appendix Two, place the sheets of paper on the floor in a circle. Explain each of the stages of grief above and have each client walk the circle explaining which stage they are experiencing currently and how they expressed grief during the past stages.

Dealing with Grief: Normal Grief vs. Complicated Loss

According to Tian Dayton, PhD, feeling grief is a "natural occurrence when we lose someone we care about . . . it is a testimony to our ability to become meaningfully attached and is not pathological or unnatural."

Complicated loss is different from normal grieving. In normal grieving, men, over time, prefer to focus on emotional issues and women focus on thinking. Unless the loss is complicated, most people work through their loss within one year to a year and a half. Clients who experience loss while in treatment benefit from having their feelings recognized and understood.

People with painful histories may find the loss of a loved one or a job hard to tolerate. They may sink into feelings of hopelessness that are more persistent than the hopeless feelings of a normal grieving process.

Sometimes a loss becomes complicated when it triggers past painful emotional states from previous losses that have gone ungrieved or were overwhelming. People who suffer from addiction and codependency may be more vulnerable because of the cumulative effect of their painful history.

Warning Signs

- Excessive guilt
- Excessive anger or sudden outbursts
- Recurring or longlasting depression
- Caretaking behavior
- Self-mutilation
- Emotional numbness
- Chronic relationship problems

Losses We Bring on Ourselves (You Cannot Say Hello until You've Said Goodbye)

Losses we bring on ourselves, such as divorce, getting sober, moving house, or sending children away to school, contain emotions that are difficult to feel and process. We may feel conflicting emotions such as sadness and joy, excitement and fear, or pain and relief. These mixed emotions can cause feelings that make the loss difficult to process. The DBT concept of thinking dialectically (see Chapter 8) encourages us to be able to hold two opposing emotions at the same time. We can feel pain at the loss of a loved one and relief that they are no longer suffering. Some of the losses we bring on ourselves include:

- The effects of divorce on spouse and children
- Family dysfunction or loss of parental attention
- Addiction: Loss of periods of time due to using and abusing substances
- Loss of addictive substance or behavior, working on sobriety and recovery

- Loss of a job, health, youth, children at home, retirement and life transitions. Sometimes, children leaving home can be a happy occasion!

When people don't spend enough time mourning a loss or discussing it with friends or relatives, it remains in unmarked graves, within our unconscious, rarely spoken about for fear of eruption. This can lead to further loss of connection with the self and intimate relationships. When we do not mourn these types of loss we may:

- Stay stuck in unresolved anger and pain which can fuel addiction and depression
- Lose access to our innermost feeling world.
- Cause trouble in relationships because we are still actively in a past relationship. with a situation or person, no longer present.
- Project an unfelt, unresolved grief onto another situation where it does not belong.
- Carry deep fears of subsequent loss or abandonment.

Exercises

Empty chair

Allow the person, situation, addiction, job, inner child, or unwanted emotion to be represented by an empty chair. This can also be done in an individual session.

Instruct the client as follows: You are invited to finally say what has been left unsaid, to express your truth and say goodbye.

Letter writing: Write a letter to the person, thing, disease or situation you feel you've lost.

Photographs: Make a collage of photographs that represent a period in your life that has passed but that you want to honor the pain of.

Discussing Grief: Pain Shared Is Diminished and Joy Shared Is Increased

Set up a spectogram on the floor with Very Much---------------Very Little
Ask: How much grief is in your life right now?
What is your level of loss?
How angry do you feel? How tired? How anxious?
How much fear do you have about your future?
How much excitement do you feel about your future?

DBT Skill: Self-Soothe

When a person is having a bad day or is under a lot of stress, he can use the self-soothe skill to help him calm down and tolerate the discomfort in a healthier way. People with addictions and trauma rarely find time to just relax in a healthy way. Some are so busy doing things for others, they fail to spend time self-soothing. Self-soothe helps a person stay grounded in the body and in the present moment and distracts him from the emotional pain he is experiencing.

To use self-soothe effectively, access all of your five senses: Vision, hearing, smell, touch, and taste. If you tend to overeat, food may not be your best choice for self-soothe.

One way to easily have access to elements for self-soothing is to create an SOS (self or soothe) box. Place objects for each of the five senses in the box so they will be readily available at all times:

> **Vision:** Look at old magazines and choose a picture that reminds you of your safe place. An imaginary spot, a river, mountain, lake, beach or meadow, say, where you could simply relax with no cares in the world and appreciate the wonders of nature.
>
> **Hearing:** Write down a list of your favorite songs and place them in the box, or leave your iPod in the box with your favorite tunes on it and listen when you need a break.
>
> **Smell:** Place scented oils or scented candle in the box.
>
> **Touch:** Put a small, soft doll or teddy bear in the box or something smooth and comfortable to the touch.
>
> **Taste:** Collect coupons for your local ice cream store and treat yourself, or simply place a small piece of chocolate, candy, or gum in the box for enjoying later.

Closing the Chapter on Grief

Use an 8½ × 11 piece of white paper and design a greeting card expressing your feelings about a loss in your life. The loss could be of a spouse, relative, parent, institution, addiction, inner child, innocence, or anything you no longer have or want. Fill in the blanks below and include the answers in your card.

- I'm sorry for _____
- Thanks for _____
- Please forgive me for _____
- I'm willing to forgive you for _____
- What I miss most about you is _____
- What I needed from you was _____
- What I got from you was _____

Closing: Your Last Day on Earth

If you knew this was your last day on earth, how would you answer the following questions:

1. What would you want to see?
2. What would you want to hear?
3. What would you want to touch or feel?
4. What would you want to taste?
5. What would you want to smell?

Allow each group member to describe these in detail.

4   The Ravages of Anger

Warm Up: Various Forms of Anger

To the facilitator: Use the worksheets in Appendix 3. Place the sheets of paper on the floor in rows. Have each client select the form of anger they are experiencing currently and how they express it in relationship to others.

As an alternative or follow up place *managing anger* sheets on the floor to present ways of managing anger in a healthy way. These could include:

- Giving the person the benefit of the doubt
- Do onto others as they want to be done unto
- Learn to become more assertive and stand up for yourself
- Radical acceptance: Accept what you cannot change
- Observing angry feelings and letting them go without taking action

Anger Map Questions

On the following page, in the center of the anger map, write a phrase that describes the main thing that makes you angry. For example, you might write: When people don't listen to me, when people cut me off in traffic, when people try to push their beliefs on me.

Write examples on the squiggly lines of actual incidents in your life where these anger-provoking occurrences happened. Process and get feedback. Or, you can continue the experiential elements of the exercise by doing the following.

Choose group members (auxiliaries) and play the scenes out, using a current example where the auxiliary plays the anger provoker and the client plays herself. Continue the dialogue until historical elements become evident and you notice a theme. Ask where she might have felt this way before?

Stop the present day example and choose new auxiliaries to play scenes from the past that may be transference onto the present or may have fueled present day anger. Play the scene out. Spiral back to present day, unfreeze it, and play it out again. After exploring the past scenario and reliving the present, do a group process asking the following questions:

1. What do you understand today that you didn't understand then?
2. What choices are you aware of now that you were unaware of then?
3. What new behaviors might you try beginning now that could affect or alter your situation?
4. What could you say to yourself then from where you stand today?

Anger Map

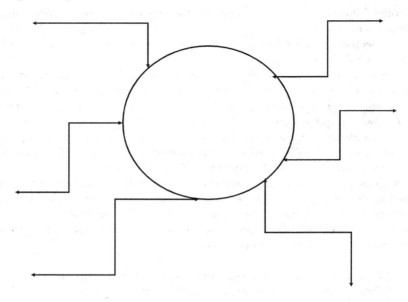

Figure 4.1 Anger Map

DBT Skill: Opposite Action

According to McKay, Wood, and Brantley (2007), our emotions are legitimate and valid and should not be ignored. It's when we react with our emotional *mind* that we have to be careful not to express our emotions in a negative way, because acting on emotions can lead to destructive consequences. Another problem with acting on emotions is that it intensifies the emotion. Instead of simply observing the emotion and letting it pass, acting on the emotion can lead to feeling consumed with anger, fear, anxiety, loneliness, or shame.

That's where opposite action comes in. Opposite action is about regulating our emotions. Being aware of what is happening in our body when we feel a certain emotion and working to calm the emotion down. According to McKay, Wood, and Brantley (2007), there are six steps to opposite action:

1. Acknowledge what you feel. Describe the emotion.
2. Ask yourself if there's a good reason to regulate or reduce the intensity of this emotion.
3. Is it overpowering? Does it drive you to do dangerous or destructive things? Is it justifiable to react in this way?
4. Notice your body language and behavior that accompanies the emotion. What's your facial expression, your posture? What are you saying and how are you saying it? What, specifically, do you do in response to the emotion?
5. Identify opposite action:

   a. Anger: How can you relax your face and body so it doesn't scream "I'm angry" or "I'm scared"? How can you acknowledge or ignore rather than attack?
   b. Depression: How can you convey confidence and vigor rather than depression?
   c. Fear: How can you move toward, not away from, what scares?

6. Fully commit to opposite action, and set a time frame to work on it. What were the consequences of acting on your emotions last time it happened? What are the possibilities that it could happen again?
7. Monitor your emotions. Notice how the original emotion may change or evolve. It helps you shift to a more appropriate reaction. Use the graph in Table 4.1 to monitor issues and how they affect your emotions. Then, after using opposite action, fill in the graph in Table 4.2 to note the change.

Table 4.1 Emotions Before Using Opposite Action

Issue	Emotion	Body Posture	Outcome

Table 4.2 Emotions After Using Opposite Action

Consequences	Change	Emotion Now	Body Posture

Opposite Action Experientially: Stand on Feelings

[Susan Woodmansee, MS, OTR, TEP, CAC 1, psychodramatist shared this exercise.]

Have laminated cards with each primary emotion (anger, sadness, shame) on them. On the back of the card, have the opposite action. Put the feeling side up and have clients stand on the emotion they have the most difficulty with. Discuss. Turn the card over and discuss which of the opposite actions the client can use successfully.

Here's how the cards read:

Anger:

> Is the anger justified and you want to change how you feel?
> Yes: Be kind, build empathy, gently avoid the person, accept the situation.
> No: Solve the problem, distract yourself, express your anger skillfully.

Sadness:

> Is the sadness justified and you want to change how you feel?
> Yes: Be active, leave your room and go for a walk, be more sociable, talk to people. Be willing to engage in life instead of avoiding it. Get dressed up and go to town.
> No: Solve the problem causing the sadness. Ask yourself, why am I holding on to this emotion? What's the benefit I'm seeking by holding on? Act in a way that gives you a true benefit.

Fear:

> Is the fear justified and you want to change how you feel?
> Yes: Solve the problem or get out of the way.
> No: Approach the situation anyway and mindfully engage until the fear dissipates.

Closing: What Are You Still Angry About?

Written exercise: Have each group participant choose two things they are currently still angry about and place each one on a 3 × 5 card.

Place a piece of painter's tape on the floor about five or six feet long to represent a spectogram, a sociometric line of measurement.

The spectogram goes from 0–100%. Let each client place her anger card at what percentage she is struggling with that anger. For example, one of the cards might be about my anger at being bullied in high school, which I place on the spectogram at 60%. Have the client stand on the 60% mark on the line and talk about her experience. As you interview her, ask what she has gained from this experience? What resources has she learned and cultivated as a result of this event? How much energy are she currently giving to this past event? What benefit does she receive from holding on to this event? What would it take for her to move down to maybe holding only 20% of the anger? Is she willing today to let it go? If so, the client tears up the 3 × 5 card and throws it in the wastebasket. If not, ask what she would need to begin to change this pattern and gain healthy energy and passion for life in the here and now?

5　The Role of Depression in Addiction and Trauma

Warm Up: The Depression Timeline

Written exercise: Draw a timeline of your depression from the earliest age you can remember until the present and any associated events that may have affected your depression. For example: Your family moved, you lost a grandparent, lost a friend or pet, any one of which was related to your becoming depressed. When finished, share your timeline with a group member and notice if there are themes, recurring events, or situations you can identify.

Theme: Depression

Fifteen million people in the USA suffer from clinical depression while 16,000 people annually commit suicide. The cause, beneath the psychological and bio-chemical causes, is a lack of appreciation for the very act of living. Depression clouds our minds with negative and self-critical shaming thoughts. There is an element of fatigue, poor concentration, irritability, and anxiety caused by passivity, inactivity, and boredom.

People contribute to their own depression with self-sabotage. If a person believes he is unworthy of success or happiness, he will subconsciously self-sabotage. The depression *danger* signs include:

- Isolating: Instead of being by yourself, seek out other people to help you.
- Inactivity: When we just sit around and think about ourselves, we focus on our shortcomings, past mistakes, few friends, the way other people have treated us, and a general sense of life not being worth living.
- Instead of asking why, ask "What can I do about it, when, who can help me, where and when do I start the process? All these questions are solvable.
- If only: Thinking *things would be better if only* . . . When we're depressed we wish things would be different. We forget mindfulness and the concept of living in the moment, one day at a time, and accepting that what is is what is supposed to be.
- Poor me: When we are unwilling to help ourselves, we strive for sympathy from others. It is usually a cover-up for resentment, anger, fear, envy, guilt, and procrastination.
- Expectations: We grow up with certain expectations that parents, teachers, and religious leaders put on us. We also put high expectations on ourselves of *what we should be accomplishing by this age*, comparing ourselves and our lack of achievement to others who *seem* to be doing so much better than we are.
- Negative self-talk: The so-called *devil on our shoulder* thrives on putting ourselves down with negative thinking. When we use words like should, must, always, and never, we are literally *"shoulding"*[1] on ourselves. Think about it. Would you allow someone else to put you down the way you put yourself down?

What's the Answer?

1. Change the channel in your head from negative to positive. Create an angel for your other shoulder, and talk back to that negative voice. If you were advising a negative friend to think more positively, what would you say?

---

[1] Albert Ellis, a US psychologist, invented this term to mean "using too many shoulds".

2. Use opposite action. Set goals for yourself, write them down, and get busy on your personal plan to achieve something that will make you feel you have a purpose.
3. Keep in contact with other people who support you.
4. Watch your health. Exercise is a natural way to fight depression. So is eating healthy foods and getting plenty of rest. Mindfulness and meditative practices such as yoga also help you focus on the present moment.

Letter From Your Depression

You ask the question; your negative voice answers:

> How did you come to be?
> Why did you start?
> What helped you? (Anxiety, relationship problems, etc.)
> What have I not wanted to face because of you in my life?

Now you answer:

> What stops you from being happier?
> What are you like when you're at your best?
> What will you feel when depression is no longer an issue?
> How will you do things differently when you have more happiness?

Feelings Inventory

Fill in the blanks:

> I needed my parents' love when I . . .
> When I am emotionally supported I can . . .
> When I feel that their love is based on my performance, I feel . . .
> In my family, success means . . .
> The price I paid for being an independent child was . . .
> The benefit I get from worrying about the future is . . .
> And that helps me because . . .
> If I change that means I will have to . . .
>
> > If I don't _____ then . . .
> > If I don't _____ then my parents will say . . .
> > When my procrastinating voice says, Oh! It'll be OK, you're fine, don't
> > worry about anything, that voice sounds like my . . .

DBT Skill: Cheerleading Statements

[Contributed and copyright by Rex Steven Sikes, IDEA Seminars, and Rex Sikes Entertainment, LLC: http://IDEA-seminars.com and http://dailyinspirationandgratitude.com.]

> What you focus on, you get. Rex Steven Sikes

In traditional DBT, cheerleading statements are positive affirmations we say to ourselves to help us boost our confidence, self-esteem, and escape the shackles of depression. Experientially, the problem is we have two voices going on in our head every moment of the day. According to Rex Sikes, originator of Directed Questions TM (1990), people who do affirmations are wasting their time, because they are setting up internal conflicts that cause them to activate the opposite of what they want! When people look into the mirror and say, "In every day and in every way, I am getting better and better," a part of their mind comes back and says, "bull!" Doesn't it? It is just like if I told you that you have a blue shirt on when you actually have a red one on! I say, "nice blue shirt" and you say, "it's not blue, it's red." Then I say, "it's blue," and you say "no, it's red" . . . we could go on like this forever . . . which is exactly what happens for most people when they do affirmations.

The science behind this concept is that the purpose of our subconscious mind is to protect us. For example, a person is driving along and there is a traffic light ahead turning orange. In our mind, we ask can I make it through the light before it turns red or should I slow down? We're always asking questions of ourselves and our subconscious protects us.

Here also, we ask questions of our subconscious mind and it searches our brain for the answer that protects us. According to Sikes, *the quality of your life depends on the quality of the questions you ask.*

Some Sample Questions

Why am I so blessed?
What new wonderful things will I discover from this group?
How can I become sober and enjoy the process?
I wonder in how many ways I can accept myself?
I wonder how quickly I can achieve emotional sobriety?
Which sensation in my body feels the very best right now?
How quickly will I begin to learn these new DBT and other skills?
How naturally and easily will I begin to pay attention to pleasant feelings?
How soon will I begin to notice with delight how happy I can become?

Have clients come up with a series of their own questions.

Closing: Facing Your future

Place a scarf or sheet representing the future on the floor. Have the client stand on the scarf and speak from the future to depression in the present:

The gift I have gained from you is_____.

If the client is not able to identify a gift, hand them the following list of factors that came out of the research:

- Relationships
- Humor
- Purpose/Passion
- Connectedness
- Inner Direction
- Independence
- Adaptability/Flexibility
- Competence
- Spirituality
- Optimism
- Renewal
- Initiative
- Morality
- Support System
- Perseverance
- Creativity
- Self-worth
- Learning
- Perceptiveness/Insight (from the International Resilience Project by Edith Brotberg)

6 Self-Regulation

Addiction Recovery

Poem: Goodbye to Addiction

By Allan J. Katz

You protected me from conflict
You soothed my shattered self,
You were my friend when I was lonely,
And when boredom came to rest.

You were my friend when lovers refused me,
You always pleased me,
At first I blamed you on pure curiosity,
Then you got the better of me.
I couldn't get enough of you,
Now I'm getting rid of you!

Goodbye addiction, you meant so much to me,
When I escaped into my fantasy world to escape my fears and
     insecurities.
Being anonymous made me feel powerful, sly and invisible,
But deep inside you ended up making me feel miserable.

I latched on to you to pass the time,
When I started new projects or just out of town,
I longed to connect to my fantasies and dreams,
And you always obliged by creating the scene.

Even in success you enveloped my life,
How could I be successful, it just didn't feel right.
With you at my side, I could feel powerful and in charge,
An excuse to procrastinate, to escape my wounded scars.

Now, as I think at all the time I've wasted,
All the real hopes and dreams that could and should have been,
I realize now that in a way you are a blessing in disguise,
Because in my desire to get rid of you,
I've come to appreciate my true self,
And know that my Higher Power is really in charge,
And all I have to do is give HIM the power to destroy you.

Warm Up: Select a Trinket

Place several toys in the center of the room, including animals, happy meal toys, and objects that will help to create imagination like masks, shields, puzzles, keys, rocks, shells, ropes, etc. Ask each participant to choose a toy that represents his addiction or medicator. If he has several ask him to pick the one that he is struggling with at present. Participants hold their toy in front of themselves and speak to an empty chair, which represents themselves, and speak as the voice of the addiction. Some possible scenarios: "I have control over you"; "You need me to function"; "You are not strong enough to fight me." This allows the participant to hear the message from the role of the other, in the here and now.

Theme: Addiction Recovery: Mindfulness vs. Distraction

The idea of being mindful is centuries old and just now coming into the mainstream of modern psychology as a tool to calm the mind and help regulate emotional turmoil. Our lives are filled with distractions so that living in the now is a difficult task indeed. Add to that the scourge of addiction, depression, and anxiety and it seems an impossible task. How can I be mindful of the present when my mind is racing with hundreds of thoughts, my past, sometimes traumatic events, and the fear of what the future will bring?

Eckhart Tolle, in his 1999 book, *The Power of Now*, explains that "all negativity is caused by an accumulation of psychological time and denial of the present." Anxiety, tension, stress, and worry are all caused by focusing too much on the future. Guilt, regret, anger, sadness, and bitterness are caused by focusing on the past and not concentrating on the present moment.

Recovery from addiction requires a focus on the present moment. It is the ultimate distraction and cannot be quenched by living in the past or worrying about the future. When you can bring your past baggage, trauma, abuse, or family roles into the present moment and deal with them, you can begin to heal and recover from addiction. By avoiding distractions and concentrating on the present, you can get a lot more work done, whether in your job or in enhancing your mental health.

Experiential therapy does exactly this. It brings past incidents into the here and now and clients are able to deal with the leftover emotions that continue to rob them of their sobriety. Our subconscious mind does not know the difference if we are speaking to the real perpetrator or a group member in the auxiliary role as perpetrator. Therefore, clients can express anger, fear, shame, and grief in a way that fosters healing and viewing situations from the perspective of the role of the other.

The Addiction Connection Dilemma

Addiction is less about seeking pleasure and more about the need to escape from the pain of the wounded soul and dissociate from the pain caused by trauma, abuse, roles, rules, and expectations. Every person craves attention, affection, and connection but people who have experienced trauma learn quickly that other people cannot be trusted. Therefore, they isolate to escape the pain of not having their emotional needs met properly.

This problem is really the solution. One of the primary means of healing from addiction is to humble ourselves and learn to depend on others who have been where we are now and can help us forge the path ahead toward emotional sobriety. We cannot do this alone. We were created for relationships and we need deep emotional bonds with people we can trust. So, while stopping the addictive behavior is the goal, in order to achieve emotional sobriety one needs to get past the fear and avoidance of being vulnerable enough to let others see the true person inside, rather than the mask we're used to wearing.

DBT Skill: Distract

Regulating emotions is difficult for people with addictions. Addicts tend to numb themselves with alcohol, drugs, gambling, sex, food, video games, and many other pleasures. They do this at even the slightest discomfort caused by anger, stress, boredom, or loneliness. The distract skill is to practice observing your feelings, thoughts, and emotions. A person does not have to act on them, just let them go like an egg flying off a frying pan. When thoughts trigger you, simply distract yourself to survive the moment without making it worse. Once a person distracts himself, the intensity of the emotion will subside when he allows it to happen. When we can solve problems, solve them. If a person can't solve the problem, survive it by distracting instead of causing more problems like shame, guilt, remorse, relationship problems, and abusing drugs.

Use the following experiential techniques for distracting yourself from emotional distress:

- Hold a piece of ice in your hand until your mind begins to move from the uncomfortably painful emotion to the discomfort of the ice. This actually works in defusing a crisis and lessening emotional turmoil.
- Go around the room and ask each person to think of a mildly stressful situation in their life. Then have each person alphabetically name a TV show, movie, play, or book. After the distraction of naming, ask the group if they can remember the stressful situation or has the intensity changed at all.

The Addiction Wheel

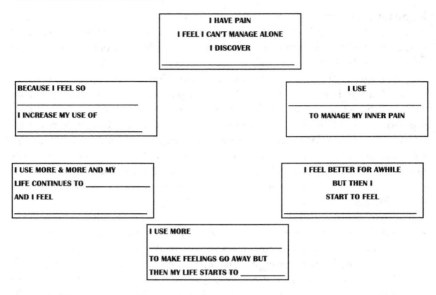

Figure 6.1 The Addiction Wheel

From Dayton, T. (2000).*Trauma and addiction*, Deerfield Beach, FL, Health Communications.

Put out sheets of paper with the words and blanks as shown above. Have each group member walk from one to another following the sequence and filling in the blanks with her own words.

Process with the group.

Closing: You Are Not Alone

Get a large sheet of butcher's paper or tape four 11 x 17 sheets of paper together to make a poster. Have the group sit around the paper on the floor and write with colored markers the type of addiction they have and the consequences of their addiction. Have each group member use a different color marker. When finished have each group member report on her addictions and the consequences. Ask other group members if they have the same addiction or consequences. If they do, have them draw a line from their list to the list of the other group member who was sharing. Process what comes up for group members when they realize they are not alone.

7 Radical Acceptance

Warm Up: Chair

Set up the room with four chair choices:

1. Two chairs set side by side
2. Two chairs back to back
3. One chair alone
4. Six to seven chairs piled in a chaotic heap

Ask each participant to choose the chair sculpt that seems to speak to them. Each person shares why he made that particular choice with the group.

DBT Skill: Radical Acceptance

This skill identifies what you have control over and what you don't have control over and knowing the difference between the two. It's a method for coping when a person is under stress. Radical acceptance is learning to be skillful enough to let things go, like your past, that you cannot change and move forward. It is not about approval or resignation. You don't have to like what happened in your past, but you do need to move forward in your life. It's the fundamental principle of Dialectical Behavior Therapy; we accept people or situations the way they are and know that there is always room for improvement.

When we have a negative emotion and we don't accept it, in other words, we are unwilling to sit with the feeling, thinking it's not helpful or its harmful, we tend to escape into behaviors like drugs, alcohol, sex, gambling, shopping, etc. to avoid the feeling. This unwillingness to sit with the feelings leads to cloudy thinking and behaviors that cause us to feel guilt and shame. It becomes a vicious cycle because, to the addict, the only way we know to get rid of stress, guilt, and shame is to numb out the feeling and use again.

By the same token, when we accept the negative emotion and can simply sit with it until it dissipates, we practice opening ourselves up to accepting the discomfort. We are willing to face the challenge and simply notice ourselves slowing down to observe our urges and bring awareness to our values, morals and beliefs.

Our emotions rise like a wave in the ocean. They peak and then fall. It's our willingness to sit with the emotion until it weakens which promotes acceptance and self-soothing.

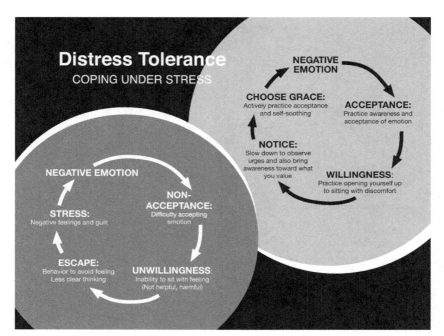

Figure 7.1 Distress Tolerance

DBT Exercise: Accepting Reality

I refuse to accept the following realities in my life today:

1.
2.
3.
4.
5.

When I refuse to accept realities, I:

1. throw a tantrum
2. give up
3. manipulate the other person until I get what I want
4. argue
5. give in
6. other _____

When I refuse to accept reality, I experience suffering by:

1.
2.
3.
4.
5.

Marsha Linehan's Four Choices of Dealing with a Problem

1. Solve the problem.
2. Accept the problem.
3. Change the problem.
4. Stay miserable.

Awareness

Lay a large sheet or scarf that represents the problem on the floor.
Give the client three options:

Option 1: I am aware of problem and working on _____. Have
them step onto sheet as they make their statement.

Option 2: I am aware of the problem. I'm thinking about it, but not
willing to take any action at this point, so I will not step on the sheet.

Option 3: I know there are issues, my family and friends continue to
remind me of them, but I am not willing to acknowledge them at this
time, in fact, I choose to look the other way.

Closing: Losing Acceptance

Note to group leader: A spectogram is a linear imaginary line drawn on the floor from one end of the room to another. One side represents zero and one side represents 100. Or you can substitute numbers for "very much" and "very little" or any other combination of extremes.

In this floor exercise, set up one side as "very much" and the other as "very little."

VERY MUCH--VERY LITTLE

Have group members stand at any point on the spectrum as you give them each one of these scenarios:

I accept other people even though I disagree with them politically
VERY MUCH--VERY LITTLE
I accept other people even though I disagree with them religiously
VERY MUCH--VERY LITTLE
I accept other people even though they may have a different sexual orientation
VERY MUCH--VERY LITTLE
I am willing to accept things I cannot change
VERY MUCH--VERY LITTLE
I am willing to trust the present moment and not worry about the future
VERY MUCH--VERY LITTLE
It's difficult to radically accept trauma that happened in my past
VERY MUCH--VERY LITTLE

Ask each group member as they stand along the line why they are standing in that position. This engenders more group cohesion in understand differing viewpoints and beliefs.

8 Forgiveness

Warm Up: Forgiveness

Place forgiveness sheets from Appendix Four lined up on the floor spread out and have each client stand on the sheet he feels is true for him. None of these is necessarily true but all are common misconceptions about forgiveness that you will dispel in the coming exercises. This chapter will concentrate on forgiveness and the DBT skill of think dialectically. You will play the angel song to get the group in the mood for forgiveness, do the forgiveness exercises and readings, and then finish the day with the Magic Shoppe, page 64.

Theme: Forgiveness

> Do as the heavens have done, forget your evil;
> With them, forgive yourself. William Shakespeare, *The Winter's Tale*

Forgive: *verb;* definition: stop blame and grant pardon. Let it go, release, absolve, accept an apology, excuse, forget, kiss and make up, let bygones be bygones.

Why is it important to forgive? Because no one in whom true forgiveness rests can suffer. Whoever forgives is healed. When you forgive, you release yourself from worldly illusions, while those who hold on to resentment and anger bind themselves to them.

Fear condemns and love forgives. Forgiveness undoes what fear has produced, returning the mind to the awareness of a Higher Power. It is how illusion disappears. Forgiveness is the great release from time. It is the key to learning that the past is over. Madness speaks no more. There is no other teacher and no other way. For what has been undone no longer is.

Forgiveness heals hurt, anger, resentment, rage, guilt, and grievances toward others and oneself. The unforgiving mind is torn with doubt, confused about itself, and all it sees, afraid and angry, weak and blustering, afraid to go ahead, afraid to stay, afraid to waken or to go to sleep, afraid of every sound, yet more afraid of stillness, terrified of darkness, yet more terrified at the approach of dawn.

The major difficulty in giving genuine forgiveness is you still believe you must forgive the truth and not illusions. You conceive of pardon as a vain attempt to look past what actually is there; to overlook the truth, in an unfounded effort to deceive yourself by making an illusion true. When your forgiveness is complete you will have full gratitude; for you will see that everything has earned the right to love by being loved, even yourself!

Stop letting your experiences of the past dictate how you respond to life today. It cannot be done without revisiting your childhood. We need to become aware, to raise our consciousness. To create a level of consciousness for ourselves that allows us to observe ourselves.

Think about and discuss the following questions:

- Why are you holding on to this form of suffering? What is its meaning to you?
- What freedom might forgiveness offer you?
- Why have I been attracted to the type of people I have had relationships with in my life?
- Why do I react certain ways in certain situations?
- Where did these behavior patterns come from?
- Why do I sometimes feel so helpless, lonely, desperate, scared, angry, suicidal?

The Forgiveness Exercise

To the therapist: Describe how all of us in life have an angel (a person in our life, we can always turn to and will give us unconditional love and advice; our personal angel). Ask each group member to identify someone in her life who is her angel. Have them get into pairs facing one another, imagining the person in front of them is her angel. As they are thinking, download or play the song "Angel" by Sarah McLachlan, and have them meditate on the concept as they listen. Process with each group member.

Have each group member select a different partner, facing each other, feet on the floor or sitting with legs crossed. When the room is quiet, give the following instructions:

1. Don't speak. Close your eyes and imagine the person sitting in front of you is the person, institution, belief, parent, teacher, friend, or value you wish to forgive. When forgiving yourself, imagine yourself as a child sitting in front of you.
2. In your mind, tell the person facing you what they did to you and you turned out because of what they did. How did you feel then when it happened and how do you feel now?
3. In your mind, tell them what your life would have been like, what you could have accomplished SOONER if this had not happened.
4. In your mind tell them what role YOU played in the way they treated you.
5. Forgive them. Say: "I forgive you. I forgive you for the pain you caused me in the past, intentionally or unintentionally, by your thoughts, actions or words. I forgive you."
6. Ask for forgiveness: "I ask for your forgiveness for anything I may have done in the past that caused you pain; by my thoughts, actions or words. Even for those things I didn't intend to cause you pain, I ask your forgiveness."
7. Allow your heart to open up to the possibility of forgiving yourself. Say: "I forgive you."

Process with each group member sharing. What came up for you? What did you relate to? How difficult or easy was it to forgive? How do you feel now?

DBT skill: Think Dialectically

The word dialectical comes from the Greek word dialectic, which means that two seemingly opposing ideas can co-exist, without diminishing one another. For instance, it is possible to want to stay sober and still want to use substances. It is possible to be sad about certain parts of your life and happy about others. It is possible to love someone and still be angry with them at the same time.

Addicts and people who experience trauma look at things in terms of black and white, right or wrong, perfect or imperfect. When they experience a negative feeling, they suddenly want to make it go away and turn to abusing substances. Instead, think dialectically and realize there are also some positive things in life you can hold onto. Actually, most of our lives we live in the gray areas. In DBT, we become willing to take our masks off and look at our life in a new and different way. It is a great relief when we realize there are alternatives to looking at our lives, our feelings, and our relationships, without having to make emotional decisions despite the consequences.

When you become triggered to use substances, think dialectically, and you will realize that you can surf your urges like a wave in ocean. The wave goes up and eventually comes down. So it is with our urges. If you can just step back and think about what else is true about the consequences of your actions. Last time I abused substances, I ended up in jail, wrecked my car, got a DUI, lost a relationship, or lost the trust of my family. Even in this moment of struggle, you can realize you have a choice. On the one hand, you want to use, while, on the other hand, you want to remain sober.

An Experientially Dialectic Magic Shoppe Variation

Anne Ancelin Schutzenberger (1966, p. 79) said that the magic shop was first used at the Moreno Institute around 1943 and developed by Hanna Weiner (New York), Leon Fine (St. Louis) and Schutzenberger herself (Paris, 1966, 1970). This is a variation that brings the concept of the dialectic to life in both a humorous and powerful way. It replicates the conversations people have in their mind when they are trying to make a decision: Should I or shouldn't I? Somatic experiential (see Chapter 16) techniques are used to give the protagonist a bodily feel for the struggle:

1. Prepare sheets of paper with large bold letters. Put the following words on each sheet: SUCCESS, BETTER RELATIONSHIP, SERENITY, COURAGE, PEACE OF MIND, HAPPINESS, ASSERTIVENESS, etc.
2. Place the sheets on a table. The group leader is the proprietor of the Magic Shoppe. You are selling the above items and group members can come up, one at a time, and "buy" one of these items. These items are bartered for what are you willing to give up to get (item). For example, a client comes up and wants to "buy" happiness. The group leader asks: What are you willing to give up to buy happiness? The client might say he is willing to give up his addiction to buy happiness. As the group leader, have group members think beyond addiction and focus more on what triggers their addiction (fear, anger, people pleasing, procrastination, perfectionism, etc.). If they cannot, using addiction as the barter is perfectly acceptable.
3. Set up three chairs with two of the chairs on the side of the third facing the third chair. The buyer sits in the third chair and there are two chairs on each side of him for each auxiliary to represent these two elements; the item he selected, *happiness*, and what he is willing to give up to get it, say, *anger*.
4. Have the protagonist choose a group member (auxiliary) for each element, *happiness* and *anger*, each sitting in one of the chairs facing him. Select two scarves or two pieces of rope and have the protagonist hold one end and the two auxiliaries holding the other end.
5. Ask the protagonist: What does happiness look like for you? This prompts the auxiliary playing "happiness" to know what to say. Then ask: How is giving up your anger going to bring you happiness?
6. Now each auxiliary takes a turn in playing the part of anger and the other happiness. As they play their part they are to pull the rope toward them slightly without jerking. *Anger* might say things like: "Come on, it's too hard to find happiness that way. How can you forgive all those people who've hurt you. I'm the way to happiness. Happiness might say, don't listen to him, he's gotten you in trouble before and he'll continue to make you miserable. If you want me you'll have to give up your anger."
7. As the director, you can prompt each side to get them used to this exchange. Once group members get the hang of it, they usually can keep the dialogue going.

8. Get the rest of the group involved by telling them they can serve as a "double" by walking to the back of the person on either side expressing their point of view: Happiness or anger to the protagonist.

9. Have anger and happiness alternate playing their parts. Allow them to talk over each other, interrupt with comments such as: Don't listen to her, you can still use and be happy, I make you happy, don't I? You, as the director, will probably have to coach each side for a while until the auxiliaries get the hang of it. Let the dialogues go on as long as possible, while encouraging other group members to get involved doubling.

10. As if this is a good place to stop. Ask the protagonist what she is feeling in her body and where in her body she feels it. Ask the protagonist which she is going to choose.

11. De-role: Have each person playing an auxiliary role say to the protagonist, I am not your anger, I'm [their name]. This is done so that the anger auxiliary is not triggering to the protagonist in the future.

12. Process with group what came up for them, what they related to, and was this realistic and how.

Closing: Self-Forgiveness Exercise

Give each participant a heart-shaped sheet of paper to hold over their heart as you guide them through this meditation: Imagine you are taking a journey through the emotional heart and the heart has the ability to release any darkness, memories of wrong behaviors, shame, and guilt onto this heart blotter paper. Play quiet music as you ask each person to walk metaphorically through their hearts as they think about things they have said that they wished they had not said, behaviors they wish they had not done, thoughts they've had that they wished they had not had. As these memories come forward, caution the clients, not to judge but to observe and to allow the darkness of their heart surface to the paper. Let their heart write its own story. Give them as much time as they need for their story to be finished. Instruct them when they feel ready to let go of the darkness, the burden, the shame, the guilt and to forgive themselves to begin to tear the sheet in very small pieces and have a waste basket nearby where they say: "Today I choose to forgive myself and set myself free."

If time permits, have group members share one sentence on how it felt to do this exercise.

9   Setting Goals

Warm Up: Your Eightieth Birthday

Group leader reads:

> Visualize your eightieth birthday. Imagine a wonderful celebration where friends, loved ones, and associates from all walks of life come to honor you. Imagine it in as much detail as possible: See the picture, hear the sounds of the people talking, and feel the sensation of being the center of attention.

See the individuals in your mind's eye as they stand, one by one, to pay tribute to you. Assume they represent roles you are now fulfilling in life, as a parent, teacher, manager, or community leader. Assume you have fulfilled these roles to the utmost of your potential:

> What would these people say? Pause.
> What qualities of character would you be remembered for? Pause.
> What outstanding contributions would they mention? Pause.
> Look around at the people there. What important difference have you made in their lives?

Group leader processes with group members.

Theme: Happiness as a Goal

We choose our joys and sorrows long before we experience them.

Kahil Gibran

You're in Las Vegas on the Strip, experiencing the flashing lights, the neon signs announcing the big entertainers, buffets covered with cheap food. You're entering an entire district of pleasure just for the taking, not to mention the casinos and the opportunity to win a fortune. Everything is structured to give you joy, the time of your life, true pleasure; *the pursuit of happiness.*

Then you enter the casino and look around. Anxious people smoking cigarettes, pulling on handles in a desperate attempt to recoup their losses. People hanging around tables with eyes glazed over, jaded and bored, throwing down cards and dice with no perception of time, space, or the *amount* of pleasure they're supposed to be having.

You sometimes feel like screaming out: "Hey! Is anyone here having a good time?"

We seek happiness through spectator sports, hobbies, technological objects, the internet, food, shopping, glamorous movie stars, entertainment, personal trainers, vintage wine, and coffee ("The Best Part of Waking Up is Folgers in your Cup").

We view happiness as an elusive goal that only the few and fortunate will ever achieve. Those who make a million dollars, weigh 110 pounds, look beautiful, own THINGS, and enjoy the gourmet life. The problem is that once the need for material possessions is filled the joy is gone. Once the plate is empty, the joy if over. Then, if you're sober and still not happy you turn to art, music, nature, beautiful objects that adorn our homes and lawns and feel a sense of belonging. But soon that fades because while you may live within view of the most beautiful mountains, they will always remain outside you. Even if you own the Mona Lisa, you will never BE the Mona Lisa because *the person who paints the picture experiences a totally different level of joy than the person who buys the picture.*

What Is the Secret of Happiness?

The essence of happiness is the experience of completion; the unrelenting search for what is missing. We are totally dependent on one another, on the physical world, and on our own Higher Power. This dependence, this inner yearning for spiritual completion, breeds *character traits* (qualities) within us such as *humility, gratitude, mutual responsibility*, and, ultimately, *JOY*.

Spirituality: *The unrelenting yearning to complete our own human character is what ultimately brings joy.*

Completion

The Awareness of What We Already Have: Appreciation

• 15 million people in the USA suffer clinical depression, 16,000 people annually commit suicide.

- The cause, beneath the psychological and biochemical causes, is a lack of appreciation for the very act of living.
- What is a life worth living look like to you?
- Children play with a toy, or eat an apple, and as soon as they see another kid with a different toy or another piece of fruit they want THAT piece or that toy instead.

The more one acknowledges that everything comes from somewhere, the lower one's appreciation threshold, and the more pleasure one takes in even the simplest gift.

Gratitude

- Recognizing the wonders of nature, a sunset, autumn leaves.
- Recognizing the good in other people
- Gratitude must be unconditional: Why thank the bus driver; it's his job?
- Appreciate the chain of events that delivered goods and services to you.
- Appreciate gifts and give gifts to others, even of your time.
- Appreciate the wonders of your own body, organs, ability to see, hear, taste, smell.

Contentment

- Being a human being instead of a human doing.
- People confuse what is urgent with what is important, and spend their entire lives running to meet deadlines.
- The idea of a period of rest to accept and celebrate the world as it is.

Achievement

- Without obstacles there is no joy in achievement.
- Set goals and work toward them instead of trying to *buy* happiness.

Boredom

- When the joy of achievement is absent.
- A lack of catalyst to stimulate action.
- Happiness comes from tackling problems and solving them, not avoiding them. This goes back to the idea of completion.

Difficulty → Challenge → Rectification = Joy

Adequacy

- When you set goals what will be your definition of success?
- What will make your life meaningful?

- Can you only be happy if you are wealthy?
- Happiness is feeling what you are doing is significant.

Even a person with no social status or money can be happy if he sees his work as important and contributive.

Quotes to Consider and Live By

Don't let the best you've ever been be the standard for the rest of your life.

I am not afraid of storms because I am learning to sail my own ship.

The happiest people don't have to have the best of everything; they just have to make the most of everything they have.

Be kind, for everyone you meet is fighting a battle!

Happiness as a Goal Exercise

Stand up and find a person in the room who you find interesting and would like to know more about, preferable someone you have *not* met or spoken to at great length. For each question, find another person and share stories based on the following questions and quotes above:

What is a life worth living look like to you? _____

_____

Name three things (people, beliefs, accomplishments) you are grateful for.

_____ _____ _____

What does being a human *being* instead of human *doing* mean to you?

_____

What are your goals in terms of humility, gratitude, personal responsibility, and finding joy? _____

_____

Name three *obstacles* you can overcome that will help bring joy into your life. _____

_____ _____

What will make your life meaningful in terms of contributing to others that will bring you joy? _____

_____

What are the challenges remaining in your life that you must conquer, complete, and overcome?

_____

_____

When will you begin? _____/_____/_____
How will you know you've overcome, completed, or conquered it? ____

_____

DBT Skill: Goal Setting: A Life Worth Living

Goal setting is a necessary element of recovery. Without goals and dreams, something to look forward to, trauma survivors and people with addictions seem to wallow in their own misery with no direction in life and nothing to look forward to achieving. It's like walking through a forest with many paths and no map.

Goals need to be specific, measurable, realistic, and timely. If you want to lose weight, saying I want to lose 30 pounds is not a clearly defined goal. Say instead, I want to lose 30 pounds in the next 5 months and I will do that by exercising for 1 hour per day and eating a low carb diet of protein and vegetables.

There are many aspects of our lives we need to set goals for. Health, spirituality, career, self-improvement, social, and family.

Life Worth Living Instructions

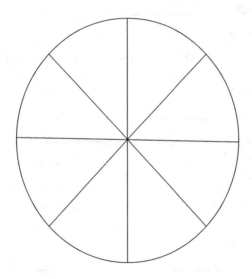

Building A Life Worth Living
Social
Recovery _____
Balance _____
DBT Other Skills _____
Short-Term Goals 6 mo–1 yr _____
Long-Term Goals 1 yr–5 yrs _____

Figure 9.1 Imagining a Life Worth Living

Work

Recovery _____

Balance _____

DBT Other Skills _____

Short-Term Goals 6 mo–1 yr _____

Long-Term Goals 1 yr–5 yrs _____

Relationships

Recovery _____

Balance _____

DBT Other Skills _____

Short-Term Goals 6 mo–1 yr _____

Long-Term Goals 1 yr–5 yrs _____

Physical Health

Recovery _____

Balance _____

DBT Other Skills _____

Short-Term Goals 6 mo–1 yr _____

Long-Term Goals 1 yr–5 yrs _____

Recreation Play

Recovery _____

Balance _____

DBT Other Skills _____

Short-Term Goals 6 mo–1 yr _____

Long-Term Goals 1 yr–5 yrs _____

Continuing Education

Recovery _____

Balance _____

Figure 9.1 (Continued)

DBT Other Skills _____

Short-Term Goals 6 mo–1 yr _____

Long-Term Goals 1 yr–5 yrs _____

Mental Health

Recovery _____

Balance _____

DBT Other Skills _____

Short-Term Goals 6 mo–1 yr _____

Long-Term Goals 1 yr–5 yrs _____

Recovery

Balance _____

DBT Other Skills _____

Short-Term Goals 6 mo–1 yr _____

Long-Term Goals 1 yr–5 yrs _____

Living, Not Just Existing ...

Considering what I have written previously, my life worth living would look like:

_____

_____

_____

_____

_____

_____

_____

_____

Figure 9.1 (Continued)

_____

_____

_____

_____

_____

Figure 9.1 (Continued)

1. Along each line of the graph write the following, one along each line. You can customize these categories according to your own personal needs:
   a. Work
   b. Play
   c. Spirituality
   d. Recovery
   e. Family/Intimate Relationships
   f. Social Relationships with Friends
   g. Physical
   h. Education

2. Put a "10" at the end of each line on the outer edge of the circle at each point.
3. Fill in the middle where all lines intersect and mark as "zero."
4. Along each line, place a dot showing how much time you spend on each of these activities on a scale of 1–10.
5. Connect the dots.
6. Using another color, place a dot on each line representing where you would like to within the next year, balancing your life toward a life worth living.
7. Connect these dots.
8. In the boxes provided above, write your goals for each category and how you plan to move from one dot to the next. For example, if you want to work less by two points so you have more time for play and relationships, what do you need to do to make this happen?
9. Write down the DBT skills you can use to accomplish these goals.
10. Share the results with your counselor and remember the SMART formula:

    S – Specific
    M – Measurable
    A – Attainable
    R – Realistic
    T – Timely

Closing: Goal Setting Experientially

Place five or six stair steps on the floor using painter's tape. Have each client write at least two or three goals for their life on a 3 x 5 card. Have clients step on stair #1 and read their goal. Continue this process for each one until their goals have been shared with the group.

Using the cards written for their life goals. Have them turn the cards over and write on the back of each goal, the beginning steps to accomplish the larger goal:

Example: Goal #1. I want to finish my degree:

Steps.
A. Research schools of choice.
B. Fill out admission and financial aid forms.
C. Research housing in area.

10 Boosting Self-Esteem with Mastery

Warm Up: Spontaneity and Creativity

Spontaneity and creativity, according to J.L. Moreno, are part of the role training for life. From the time we are born, we are confronted with new experiences. Spontaneity training is a way to enhance a person's approach to living more fully, joyfully, and connectedly. "Spontaneity is an adequate response to a new situation or a new and appropriate response to an old situation."

"Creativity is how we reshape the new thought and give it form." The first is thinking, the other is doing. Change happens when they come together, giving shape, form, and action to bring it to life.

Draw a large circle on the floor with a horizontal line through the middle. The circle represents their spontaneity, and the line represents their creativity. Have the client walk around the circle and talk about one idea he has been wanting to accomplish. Have him continue this walk until he is in touch with his longing and the body warms up to the idea. Then have him stand where the line intersects the circle and talk about if he allowed his creativity to engage with his thoughts, what would evolve. Director needs to be aware of negative messages here and encourage client to stay in creativity role. This allows the client to stay in role training to practice and create new solutions. Share this with the group and receive feedback.

Theme: Self-Esteem

Acknowledging our strengths is difficult for trauma survivors and people with addictions. We have been numbing our feelings for so long that we don't even realize we have strengths. When we've lived with criticism, unrealistic expectations coupled with abuse and trauma, our self-esteem is so low, we feel helpless about crawling out of our shell and facing reality.

However, boosting our self-esteem is necessary to lead an emotionally sober life. The DBT skill of build mastery is finding something you're good at and mastering it, which builds your self-esteem. A person becomes more confident in her own abilities when she attempts to complete a task, use a skill, or be the best person she can be. This realization of our strengths helps balance out negative feedback, judgments, and comparing others and gives us a better ability to deal with regulating our emotions more skillfully.

As you begin to master a task, keep in mind that this is a very personal exercise. What may be mastery for you may not be for someone else. Don't get caught up in judgments and comparing yourself to others. Some examples might be joining a gym, doing a 1000-piece puzzle, mastering a video game, learning a foreign language, pushing yourself to do something you've been procrastinating about, start a gratitude journal, join a social club. Remember that happiness is a journey, not a destination. To recover from trauma, find something you can focus on today, to live for, to cherish, to accomplish, to give your life meaning and make your life worth living for.

DBT Skill: Building Mastery Experientially

Ways I can build mastery:

1. _____
2. _____
3. _____
4. _____
5. _____

One thing I feel:

One thing I am good at is _____
I feel ashamed when _____
I feel good about myself when _____
Life is so wonderful when _____
I'm really good at _____
I feel proud about _____
If I thought about what I could mastery, I'd _____
It always feels good when I _____
I can_____
I will _____
I am _____
I am grateful for _____ _____ _____
I am most happy when _____

Group Mastery Exercise

1. Have each group member explain some skill they have mastered to the other group members. It can be a job skill, hobby, physical, sports. Have them go into detail about what it took to achieve mastery in this skill, the challenges they faced and how they overcame them.

2. Have group members act out, without words, one of their strengths and one of their weaknesses and see if other group members can identify them.

3. Print the following cards from Appendix Five and place on the floor. Have the group members stand on the situations in their life that prevents them from building mastery. Ask each person why they are standing there and what will it take to overcome this barrier.

Process with entire group after everyone has shared.

PERFECTIONISM
RELAPSE
DISTRACTIONS
PROCRASTINATION
UNHEALTHY EATING
LACK OF EXERCISE
LACK OF SKILLS

Three Circle Plan

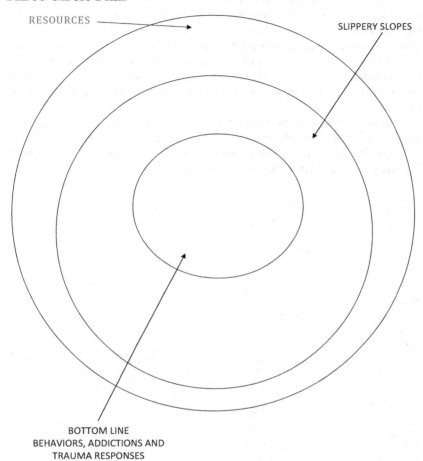

Figure 10.1 Three Circle Plan

To build mastery in recovery, it is necessary to identify core addictions and traumas that you need to eliminate. It is also essential to be able to identify slippery slopes; those behaviors we engage in which lead us to acting out or relapsing and the resources needed to help us when we feel triggered, restless, irritable and discontent. Write in the three circles in Figure 10.1 the following:

BOTTOM LINE BEHAVIORS, ADDICTIONS AND TRAUMA RESPONSES

Bottom line behaviors are those behaviors you want to stop doing and get rid of. These might include addictions, trauma responses, and character traits you want to improve on.

Slippery slopes are rationalizations we make that convince us we can still engage in behaviors that in the past have caused us to slip or relapse and end up crossing our bottom lines. For example, a person who has a problem with looking at inappropriate images online might convince himself that he can continue to look at videos that portray scantily clad individuals and say to himself: At least I'm not looking at porn. This is a slippery slope because a great deal of the time, people end up breaking their bottom lines eventually when they are triggered by slippery slopes.

Resources are the tools and skills we use so that we don't fall down the slippery slope. These might include going to 12-step groups, getting a sponsor, working the steps, learning and implementing DBT skills for emotion regulation, reading, individual, and group therapy and online websites, apps, podcasts, etc.

Closing: Resilience Factors

Have each client make a list of the following resources to remind them they are not alone, and they are gifted for problem solving:

I HAVE: External supports and resources.

Ex. People I trust, people to teach me

I AM: Inner personal strengths.

Ex. Glad to be helpful to others, hopeful

I CAN: Interpersonal skills.

Ex. Finds ways to solve problems I face

11 Relapse Prevention

Warm Up: Addiction and Recovery

Place two chairs approximately 8-10 feet apart. Label one chair "addiction" and the other chair "recovery" Have the client sit in addiction chair and describe feelings and behaviors while using. Have a group member write this on a white board for group members to view and to contribute their input. Client then moves across the room and sits in recovery chair and describes feelings, and behaviors. This is also displayed on the board for group to see and contribute. Have client move back to addiction chair and set up their recovery process. Examples being acceptance, meetings, sponsor, 12 steps, prayer, meditation, readings, asking for help, etc. For each tool have a person stand and hold a scarf as the client installs his program moving toward recovery with each tool. Finally, client has arrived at their recovery and when they look back can only see individuals holding scarves, not their addiction. Note: The more tools and resources one has the farther away they are from their addiction. This is a good teaching moment about connecting with others, asking for help, and commitment. Director asks client to relapse as he thinks out loud and dismantles his program. You might hear, I hate those meetings, it feels like everyone drank the cool aid, I think it might be a cult, I refuse to listen to my sponsor, he's as crazy as I am, etc. Relapse does not just happen it is slowly dismantled by one's thinking. Have client put program back in place making a statement of commitment. If there is one area of the program that client struggles with have them role reverse with that area to discover the issue. Usually it is with sponsor or spiritual aspects of the program where they are unwilling to ask for help or acknowledge they cannot do it alone. This time with program in place have auxiliaries drop their scarves and client can see their program is people.

DBT Skill: Play the Tape Out

One of the most effective techniques for not reacting to emotional distress is the skill of play the tape out. Think of the tape as the progression of time which led to a slip or relapse. Sometimes it can be a matter of hours, days, or months when we begin to feel disconnected from ourselves, disconnected from reality because of being restless, irritable or discontent with life. When we play the tape out in our mind, we discover that things didn't turn out so well after we slipped or relapsed and we are back to square one, starting over again. So, we might say to ourselves, *do I really want to go back to feeling withdrawals, going back to treatment, getting another DUI, suffering DTs again? Is it worth it for a moments pleasure to experience the pain in the future?*

Play the tape out can be used in the positive sense also. After someone has had a long lasting sobriety and become triggered, they can think about how good it felt to be sober and whether they really want to go back to living life in their car or on the streets.

Exercise

What would be your scenario to play the tape out that would prevent you from relapse?

_____

_____

What positive scenario can you envision from your sobriety that would help you?

_____

_____

The Relapse Trail©: A Structured and Directive Psychodrama

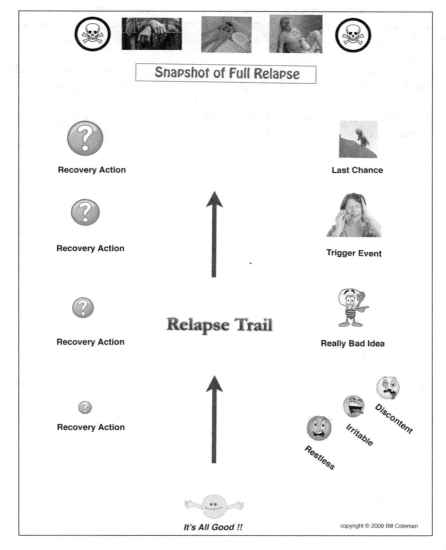

Figure 11.1 Relapse Trail

[Contributed by Bill Coleman, MSW, TEP.]

Each of Bill Coleman's exercises is newly updated with additional material and can be found in the full length book, *The Illustrated Guide to Psychodrama*, copyrighted, imprint 2017, to be published in early 2018. For further information, please visit www.cwcolemanbooks.com and/or contact him by email at coleman151@mac.com.

The Relapse Trail© is about recognizing the triggers of relapse and developing resources for recovery. It can be used for substance abuse, process addictions, eating disorders, depression, and trauma. It can be done in individual session using props but is much more impactful if done with a larger group of, say, 10–15 people. It is best done in a large room of 20 x 40 feet and is suitable for inpatient and outpatient settings.

The exercise begins by selecting a protagonist (the group member who will "do the work" and walk the trail). This exercise is best used with a group member who is set to discharge soon. Its purpose is to teach group members how to build recovery resources and the obstacles that get in the way. It is also a last chance for the protagonist to practice relapse prevention techniques in the here and now.

Step by Step Instructions for the Relapse Trail©

1. Imagine a line in the center of the room. At the end of this line have the protagonist create his worst relapse. If you have dolls, scarves, sheets, rope, etc. use these to help him set the scene.

2. Have the protagonist move to the other end of the room. Instruct the group, or ask them, what are the three things that make us vulnerable to relapse. It could happen over a period of hours, days, weeks, or months but when these emotions build up, we are at a greater risk for relapse. The three are restless, irritable, and discontent (RID). Have the protagonist select three people, each to represent restless, irritable, and discontent. Have them stand to the protagonist's right toward the worst relapse. Ask the protagonist to explain to each of these individuals what it means to him to be restless, irritable, and discontent. Have the auxiliaries repeat back or act restless or irritable or discontent.

3. Repeat that the protagonist is feeling RID and is getting closer to his worst relapse unless he gets some help. Have the protagonist select a group member as a friend or sponsor. Instruct the protagonist to tell the friend or sponsor (auxiliary) that he is feeling RID and needs his help. Call him up on the phone and see if he can come over. Instruct the protagonist that he didn't answer the phone, so now you're RID and have no one to help. So tell the protagonist that now he has made a bad decision and must pick someone to represent that bad decision. Instruct the "bad decision" auxiliary to act like a person selling the protagonist's drug of choice. Repeat to the protagonist that he is RID with no help at hand and now he makes a bad decision to call his dealer.

4. Tell the protagonist that if we wants to stay sober and not have his worst relapse, he had better call someone to go to a meeting. Choose someone in the group to take him to a meeting. Ask the auxiliary what time the meeting is. Whatever time they say, tell them, sorry the meeting was an hour earlier and you missed it.

5. So now you're RID, have made a bad decision, are walking closer and closer to your worst relapse, and you have no one to turn to for help. Tell the protagonist that he just received some bad news and choose someone to play bad news. Instruct the auxiliary "bad news" to say: "Your _____ is in the hospital." Now you are RID, you've made a bad decision, have no one to turn to, and now you get bad news, inching ever closer to your worst relapse.

6. Ask the protagonist who is his last resource to turn to before he relapses. Usually, hopefully, they will say their Higher Power. Ask the protagonist to choose someone to play the Higher Power. When chosen, ask the protagonist how he prays (kneeling, standing, with hands, etc.) and to approach his Higher Power and ask for help. Role reverse the protagonist with the Higher Power and have the auxiliary repeat what the protagonist

said. Then the protagonist in the reversal role as the Higher Power answers back. You can continue to role reverse or end here.

7. Have everyone return to their seats and process what came up for the group, whether you participated or not and did it seem realistic.

Experiential DBT Chain Analysis

The chain analysis was developed by Marsha M. Linehan as a visual way to describe the chain of events that leads to problem behaviors and to understand it more thoroughly, both for the client and the therapist. It is usually shown on the whiteboard in the following way:

Vulnerability: Different factors make us more vulnerable to engaging in problem behaviors after a prompting event. These can include illness, misuse of drugs or alcohol, anxiety, sadness, anger, fear, loneliness, boredom, or past event flashbacks or thoughts.

Prompting event: Describe the prompting event that started the chain reaction. What were you feeling right before the prompting event? What were you doing right before the event? Why did this problem happen today and not yesterday?

Chain of events: People don't get up in the morning saying they are going to relapse. The chain of events can happen over a period of hours, days, weeks, or months, slowing causing restlessness, irritability, and discontentment. After the vulnerability and prompting event, what was the chain of events that led to the problem behavior? What feelings, thoughts, images, occurrences were happening in your environment that kept the chain going? Describe the sequence of steps in detail. What caused the specific thought, feeling, or emotion that prompted the chain of events? What skills could have been used to stop the action at this point (distract, wise mind, observe, play the tape out, etc.)?

Problem behavior: What was the specific problem behavior (overeating, throwing a tantrum, yelling at a child, refusing to listen when told what to do, relapsing on alcohol or illicit drugs)? Describe what you did in detail.

Consequences: List the consequences of the problem behavior toward yourself, your family, your spouse, your job, your standing in social or religious circles. How did you feel after you engaged in the behavior? What would your family think if they found you engaging in this behavior? What action might they take?

Action: Think about a positive behavior or skill you could have used instead to deter the consequences. What could you have done differently?

Moving into experiential chain analysis: To get your group involved experientially, simply assign a group member to each element of the chain; vulnerability, problem, chain of events, consequences, skills needed to break the chain. Have the protagonist stand in the problem behavior position and other group members in the various other spots as per the diagram in Figure 11.1. Have the protagonist describe the problem behavior in detail, move along the chain beginning at vulnerability. Have each group member ask questions pertaining to where they are standing. When everyone has asked questions and the protagonist has answered, have the protagonist step out of the scene and have another group member act as a double, while the protagonist watches. Move the double along the chain beginning at vulnerability as each group member makes a statement describing or acting out the feeling, thought or behavior that moved the chain forward. Have other group members play a DBT skill that could have been used to block the chain of events and mediate the consequences. Process with the group. Ask each group member what it felt like playing their part. What did they relate to and did the exercise seem realistic to them? Ask group members to identify what happens to them in this process and what can be done to make it stronger.

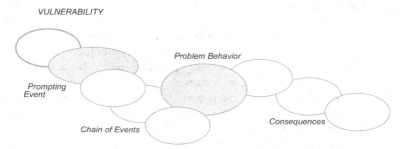

Figure 11.2 Experiential DBT Chain Analysis

Closing: Maintaining Recovery

Place two or three scarves on the floor to represent 6 months, 1 year, and 2 years in the future.

Challenge clients with the following statement. You have maintained your recovery for 6 months; as you stand on that scarf tell us how you feel, what you are doing, and who is with you. Move client to 1-year, and then 2-year space and have them share.

12 Time Management

Warm Up: Clock on the Floor

Design a big clock on the floor by laying down the following numbers 12, 3, 6, and 9 in a circle representing time. Have the client walk the clock for the past 24 hours and talk about how they managed their time. If they had to do it over, where would they save time, and how would they like to repurpose this precious commodity. Have a group member write their response on a 3 × 5 card and give it to them to remind them of their truth.

DBT Skill: Participate

Participate is all about creating a life worth living. For many of us, the fear of failure and fear of success get in the way and we end up sitting on the sidelines of life, wallowing in self-pity. Actually, it is easier to jump right in to life than to sit on the sidelines doing nothing.

Consider this: There is no such thing as failure! Everything we do is a learning experience. And fear of success? We fear success because we've been told that we're not good enough anyway, so why bother trying. How can I be a successful person if I've been told my whole life nothing I do is good enough? In actuality, perfection is an illusion of high expectations we set up for ourselves or set up for us by parents, teachers, and spiritual leaders.

In baseball, a successful hitter has a batting average of .300. That means the player only gets a hit one out of three times. In other words, he gets out two out of three times, and yet, we consider him a successful hitter. The reason, aside from the fact the pitcher is throwing balls at close to 100 miles per hour, is that facing each new pitcher is a different learning experience. It takes time, effort, and a lesson or two in striking out to perfect his batting style against that pitcher.

Participate in some worthwhile endeavor every day, whether in your work, volunteering, creating and building something with your hands, helping others, attending 12-step and other self-help meetings, pitching in and helping set up the room, brew coffee, or simply working on your hobby. What does your life worth living look like? What can you do tomorrow that will make your life closer to a life worth living?

A Life Worth Living

Where I am today	What's in the way	Where I want to be

1. Take an 8½ × 11 sheet of blank white paper and fold it into three sections as shown above. Have a set of colored markers or crayons ready.
2. You want to access the right brain so ask clients to DRAW a symbol, picture, or color to represent where they are today, where they want to be in the future and what is getting in the way. They do not have to write the titles to each section as shown above.
3. Instruct clients to think in terms of using metaphors, symbols or colors to represent each section. Encourage them to think beyond addiction and trauma and more about what is behind their using alcohol or drugs.
4. Have each group member share what they've written showing the rest of the group their drawings. Share and process.

Participate in Pleasurable Activities

Take a bath	Jog
Write down goals	Go on a date
Collect colorful rocks	Take a mini vacation
Make soup from scratch	Do yoga
Listen to funny videos	Play your favorite music
Read a book	Do odd jobs around the house
Tend to your plants	Buy a greeting card and send it to a friend
Go swimming	Buy something you've always wanted for yourself
Do a 1000-piece puzzle	Take music lessons
Forgive yourself	Forgive others
Give charity	Give people the benefit of the doubt
Participate in sports	Attend a ball game
Hold hands	Watch a movie
Crossword puzzle	Play with a pet
Acting	Meditate
Get a massage	Sit in a café and relax
Call an old friend	Take a class at the community college
Plan a yard sale	Sell things you don't need online
Start a recovery blog	Take a nap

Write your own:

_____

_____   _____

_____   _____

Time Management

Table 12.1 Time Management Grid

IMPORTANT	NOT IMPORTANT NOW
CRITICAL	
NOT CRITICAL	

In Table 12.1, fill in tasks that have to be done today that may be important or not so important. Then fill in tasks that do not have to be done today that may be important in the future or not. Use the ABC guide below to make your decisions:

A. if not done today there may be consequences
B. needs to be done in the next few days or it will become an A
C. it would be nice to get done because it bothers me but it is not essential

The Recovery Approach to Time Management and Goal Setting

	Today	1 year from now	5 years from now
1 Physical			
2 Spiritual			
3 Mental			
4 Social skills			
5 Work/school			
6 Recovery			
7 Relationships			
8 Healthy fun			

Self-awareness is the focus of the recovery movement. The DBT skill of observe helps us remain self-aware of our thoughts and feelings without having to act on them; simply being conscious of the fact that *now I'm having sad thoughts, happy thoughts, angry thoughts or shameful thoughts*, and I can let them go without acting on them.

Conscience is the focus of religion, morality, ethics, and questions of right and wrong. Our conscience is like a barometer of the soul intrinsically guiding our actions based on our thoughts and feelings. When a person behaves against his own values he feels a sense of shame and guilt. These very powerful emotions can also aid a person by being a deterrent to further behaviors against our values. (See Chapter 19.)

Independent will is will power, white knuckling our way through life. No pain, no gain.

Creative imagination is the focus of visualization and mind power. See Chapters13 and 14.

Answer the following questions:

1. What's most important? _____
2. What's healthy that gives your life meaning? _____
3. What do you want to be and do in your life?_____
4. How would you spend today, 1 year, 5 years, if that's how long you had to live? _____
5. How would I feel about life if I knew my ultimate purpose? _____
    _____

6.   How are the roles I play important to fulfilling my mission? _____

7.   What character qualities would you like to be remembered for? _____

8.   Who has made an important difference in your life and future? _____

My Mission Statement

Closing: Your Last Day on Earth

If you knew this were your last day on earth write a letter to those you leave behind telling them what you wished they knew and understood about you. Write down all the lies you have told yourself about you and others, so you will know you left this world telling your truth, and understanding that time can be your friend to change your world, by taking action.

Figure 12.1 Time Can Be Your Friend

13 Mindfulness

Using Mindfulness to Cope with Thoughts, Feelings, and Behaviors

Be still and know.

Being mindful of our thoughts, feelings and behaviors is what sets DBT apart from CBT (Cognitive Behavioral Therapy). Best practice is to begin each group session with a mindfulness exercise. Meditation is a form of mindfulness, but mindfulness on its own is about staying focused on what we are doing in the present moment. With mindfulness, we can gain an appreciation for each moment of our lives and find meaning in even the simplest experiences.

As we become more proficient at using mindfulness, we can learn to be mindful of our thoughts and feelings, to become observers, and subsequently more accepting of others who might have differing viewpoints. This results in less stress, and increases our level of appreciation for things we take for granted, and for life itself.

With mindfulness, even the most disturbing sensations, feelings, thoughts, and experiences can simply be observed and not acted on, like an egg smoothly leaving a frying pan with a Teflon coating.

We can be mindful in times of distress, by looking at the actual experience as an objective observer, using mindful breathing, and concentrating attention on the body's experience, listening to the distressing thoughts mindfully, recognizing them as merely thoughts, focusing on them, without believing them or arguing with them. If thoughts become too strong, we can focus on our breath, our bodily sensations, or create a mindful visualization of a safe place where we can escape in our mind and bring stress down to a normal level.

Jon Kabat-Zinn uses the example of waves to help explain mindfulness. Think of your mind as the surface of a lake or ocean. There are always waves on the water, sometimes big, sometimes small. The water's waves are caused by the winds, which come and go and vary in direction and intensity, just as do the winds of stress and change in our mind. It's possible to find shelter from the waves of emotions that agitate the mind. While we might try to prevent them, the winds of life and of the mind will continue to blow, with or without us.

Warm Up: Exercise in Gentle Eating

Make sure the room is quiet so client can focus.

Give each client a raisin and let them chew and eat as they normally would. Take a few minutes and walk them through a relaxation technique with deep breathing and being mindful to relax each body part starting at the head and ending with the feet.

Now, give each one a raisin but ask them to hold the raisin in their mouth, and explore its shape, size, and texture. Have them very slowly begin to bite into the raisin, being intentional in chewing slowly and chewing 20–25 times before they swallow. Have the group compare and share the two experiences.

DBT Skill: Wise Mind/Clean Mind

The DBT skill of wise mind is about integrating our emotional mind with our logical mind tapping into our intuition of what we call a *gut feeling*. You know you are accessing your intuition when there is no small voice telling you it won't work.

We have three parts to our mind. The logical part of our mind, the emotional part, and the wise part. When we make decisions with our emotional mind we make rash, impulsive, split-second decisions without thinking about the consequences. We want instant gratification and ignore what may have happened last time we gave in to our impulses. Acting impulsively leads to out of control behaviors that create chaos, destroy trust, and we coudld end up in jail, getting a DUI, sick from an overdose, or even dead. Logical mind is the part of our mind that is reasonable and rational. People who are more logical minded think in terms of facts, figures, cause and effect. This is important in learning skills and making more informed decisions. It is much easier when you are sober and healthy because when you're sick, tired, lonely, or scared, your emotional mind takes over. The problem is, acting with only our logical mind leaves out the emotional element and we need both to make intuitive decisions.

For example, say a matchmaker approaches you and tells you about a person who is about the same height as you, same religion, same city, same interests. Acting on your logical mind, it seems you might want to go out on a date with this person to get to know them better. However, you meet the person and there is no chemistry, you cannot stand their personality. So without the emotional side, deciding based just on logic is not a wise decision.

Wise mind is where a person is focused on solving problems using their intuition or gut feelings. It's where we let our logical mind evaluate what our emotional mind is thinking about doing and solving the problem.

Teaching Wise Mind Experientially

To teach wise mind experientially, set up three chairs in a row and stand behind them. The chair on the left is emotional mind, the middle chair is wise mind, and the logical chair is the one on the right. Stand in front of the emotional mind chair and explain what emotional mind is per the article above. Ask the group what happens when a person only uses their emotional mind. What type of decisions do they make? Have each group member come up, sit in the chair and say how they react with their emotional mind. Stand behind the logical chair and explain the logical side using the dating analogy. Ask each group member to come up, sit in this chair, and explain how just using logic has gotten them in trouble. Then move to wise mind and explain how intuition works and how we know when we're using our wise mind to make better decisions. It's really a problem-solving tool. For example, when a person is triggered to act out, they can step back before acting impulsively and ask themselves: Am I using my wise mind right now?

After explaining the three chairs, present the following scenario. A teenager walks into the kitchen and decides to make a milk shake. He puts the ice cream, milk, ice, syrup, and fruit into the blender and turns it on. He forgets to put the top on the blender and it splatters all over the kitchen walls, floor, counters, and makes a huge mess. Suddenly, his mother walks in and reacts using her emotional mind. Have each group member come up, sit in the chair, and speak with their emotional mind as the mother. Repeat for the logical mind chair. (It has to be cleaned up and you need to clean it up. If you're a nice parent you might help them since it was an accident.) Then ask each group member to come up and sit in the wise mind chair and speak from the wise mind position. (For example, I realize this was an accident and it has to be cleaned up. We want to teach the teenager that there are consequences to his actions even if it were an accident.)

DBT Skill: Clear Mind/Clean Mind

Clear mind/clean mind is an addiction adaptation of the DBT skill of wise mind. When we use our addict mind, similar to emotional mind, we rationalize our behavior and think we can have one more drink, no one will know, you can still hide it, you can still hang out with friends who still drink. Addict mind is how we think as addicts with all the rationalizations, excuses, lies to ourselves and others, and minimization of consequences.

Clean mind explores our thinking when we are clean and sober. Yet some of these thoughts still pop up in our minds telling us we've got this, I don't need to go to meetings anymore, I can keep paraphernalia around the house with my liquor bottles and I won't touch them! These thoughts become slippery slopes that start out as logically innocent beliefs we rationalize, then turn to disaster when we give in to the urges or get triggered.

Clear mind is the combination of addict and clean mind. You're clean, but it's very clear you could relapse. Put another way, clear mind equals setting boundaries to not fall into slippery slopes PLUS going to war against urges.

Clean Mind	Clear Mind
Now that I've been to treatment,	
I've got this and can recovery myself	_____
I can still hang out with my using friends	_____
I can keep that old pipe in the house	_____
Carrying a lot of money around is no big deal	_____
One more time won't hurt anyone	_____
12-step meetings are a waste of time	_____

Telling the Trauma Story

Set up three chairs facing one chair. Ask a group member to come up and tell his trauma story. Have the volunteer choose three people to sit in the chairs facing him. Make three signs: FACTS, FEELINGS, BELIEFS/VALUES. Ask the group member to tell his story and have each one of the three write down facts, feelings, and beliefs/values based on what they've heard from the trauma story. After the story is finished have each one of the three repeat back facts, feelings and beliefs/values.

Process with the group about what came up for them, what did they relate to and if they have anything to add to facts, feelings, or beliefs after listening to the story.

Closing: Meditations

Hand out meditations for the next 5 days and challenge clients to read one a day. Have them sit quietly and journal about what they read and its message to them. Client can also journal any changes in their perceptions and feelings. This could be shared at a later group or in individual session.

Have client tell a short three-sentence story of a precious moment in their lives when they felt excited, at peace, and accomplished. It might have been the birth of a child, a major accomplishment on the job, or school, etc. Choose someone to be you and get help from the group to re-enact the three-sentence story as the protagonist observes. This is usually a combination of the emotional brain, wise brain, and logical brain.

14 Meditation

Warm Up: Meditation

Use a locogram (a diagram done in action that represents a place or category) with the following labels printed on 8½ x 11 sheets of paper in landscape mode. Ask clients to choose one they need to meditate on to contemplate change.

Labels are placed randomly on the floor around the room. See Appendix Six for labels you can print:

Emotions
Work
Self-Care
Relationships
Spirituality
Other

Have clients share what is coming up for them regarding their choice. Encourage them to share their barriers.

DBT Mindfulness Meditation

By Allan Katz

Note to counselor: This meditation is full of hypnotic language, so it is necessary to begin the exercise with some simple breathing, noticing the coolness of the breath as they breathe in and the warmth of the breath as they breathe out. You may want to have them imagine a soft, white cloud entering their brain, and moving down the body, limb by limb, organ by organ, loosening the tightness, smoothing out the muscles and tendons and relaxing. Then, when the group is mindfully meditating, introduce the following slowly, pausing a few seconds at each ellipse:

I wonder how quickly and easily you will become aware of how mindful you can truly become . . . to concentrate on your breath, and in the unlikely event your mind drifts away into the past or into the future, how easily you bring it back into focus in your mind's eye as you continue to concentrate on your breathing . . . I want you to STOP and consider enjoying this new feeling of calmness as you listen to my voice guide you . . . so that now and in the future you can remain mindful of what is going on around you and bring your feelings and emotions into your awareness easily and naturally . . . and when you do you might notice how naturally and easily one might experience unlimited pleasure. Have you ever imagined what your life would be like if you could naturally use these DBT skills when your feelings were less than perfect? Naturally, I am sure you are aware that this experience can bring you unlimited amounts of joy and excitement beyond what you could ever imagine yourself as you move beyond any limitations and begin to expand your skills until they delight you, using them to easily reach your full potential, make new healthy choices and connections . . . and in the days and weeks and months ahead become mindful – STOP – Get a hold of yourself – and remember, the memory may not STOP the hurt BUT it can START the healing. When you say to yourself, I wonder how free I will be when I let go of resentments? How delighted will I be when I realize I have a choice to be RIGHT or to be HAPPY and I choose to be happy.

Begin to realize that most people fail to realize that their feelings toward others are determined by their feelings toward themselves and there is no reason to be afraid of storms because you are learning through these skills how to sail your own ship riding the waves of your emotions until they simply and easily fade away into the wind.

And now, you might want to imagine walking up a stairway, and with every step up you become a little more awake, a little more aware of the energy in this room surrounded by the other group members. When I count to 10 you can simply open your eyes and come back into the room. 1-2-3 beginning to wiggle your fingers and toes; 4-5-6 beginning to feel a sense of being awake and present; 7-8 being mindful of the energy in the room, feeling willing and alive; 9-10 you may open your eyes and come back into the room.

DBT Skill: One Mindful

One mindful is the opposite of multitasking. This skill trains the brain to focus on one thing at a time. It is a great skill for people whose minds are constantly racing with thoughts, feelings, worries, and anxiety. When a person concentrates on one thing at a time with awareness, he focuses his mind, body, effort, and attention on what he is doing in the present moment. This trains the brain now to relive the past or worry about the future. For example, when you're eating breakfast, instead of reading the newspaper, looking at the cellphone, listening to TV or radio, concentrate on what you're eating. Become aware of the smells of the fresh coffee brewing, the crunch of your cereal, the tastes and textures that make what you're experiencing unique.

You can also be one mindful when you're with another person. Instead of each of you separately texting people on your cellphones, be mindful of the person you're with, what they are saying, their body language, and their values, beliefs, and preferences.

One of the most effective ways to use this skill is in observing your thoughts and feelings; being mindful that you're having angry thoughts, fearful feelings, shameful thoughts, and so on and figuring out what happened before these thoughts that may be causing them.

The reason one mindful is so effective is that you are more effective when you're doing one thing at a time instead of multitasking. When a person multi-tasks, she adds stress, doubt and disorganized thought to the process and results suffer. Cherishing the moment and making the most of each experience makes our lives more meaningful.

DBT Experiential Exercise: Turning the Mind

The purpose of our subconscious mind is to protect us. When we experience emotional pain, our minds attempt to figure out a way out of it by flooding our brain with worries, negativity, frustration, disappointments, and regrets. Emotional pain cannot be solved as simply as a math problem or a business decision. We cannot think our way out of emotional pain but we can turn our minds away from the pain, focused on a more balanced state of mind.

Answer the following questions:

How strongly do you want to reduce frustration and negativity from your life?
What are you thinking about right now? Don't repress it, observe the thought.

Admit what you are focusing on and let it go of what is right or wrong, good or bad. Instead, simply notice what you are focusing on and turn your mind to a positive experience you once had, a pet, something you're grateful for. Engage all of your senses in turning the mind toward beautiful sights and sounds, delicious tastes, savory smells, and beautiful music.

You are not overpowering your emotions, you are just acknowledging what you're feeling and making an effort to turn your mind away from it and onto something more positive.

Write a paragraph about a positive experience you once had and share it with the group. You can use this to turn your mind toward this experience when you're feeling distress.

Closing: Hope for the Future

Place a scarf on the floor to represent a future projection (hope longed for in the future) and ask the client to stand in that place and talk about the area of concern from the warm up (emotions, work, self-care, relationships, spirituality, other). Now, after the teaching, how will they make one or more practical changes to move toward the future? Have him stand with his eyes closed and project what that change would look like, feel like, and how his life might shift for the good. Leader can encourage the client to speak from this place and describe what he sees, how he feels, and what has changed in his life. This somatic experience helps promote change.

15 Interpersonal Effectiveness

Interpersonal Effectiveness: DISC theory

DISC theory was introduced in 1928, in William Moulton Marston's book, *Emotions of Normal People*, later republished in 2002 by Routledge. His DISC theory explores how people behave in work and social situations and divides people into four categories. This theory is helpful in learning how and why people behave in a certain way and adapting our own style of communication to build rapport with others based on their behavior. When a person understands why a person acts in a certain way, which is neither right or wrong, they are less stressed out and more accepting of the differences of others.

D stands for direct. These are people who believe they can control their environment and they do so by saying what's on their mind. They are fast paced, task-oriented people who like to take decisive action, create change, get results, and take risks. They can be perceived as impatient, stubborn, harsh, or blunt. Direct people are "bottom line" oriented. They want to just know the bottom line, not laced with stories, examples or facts. Their greatest fear is being taken advantage of. Under pressure they are autocratic, aggressive, and demanding. They love challenges, change, and choices.

I stands for influential. These are very outgoing, inspiring people who feel they can control their environment by their enthusiastic personality. They are fun-loving, sociable people who are emotional, optimistic, and good communicators. Think of your typical salesperson! However, influential people are often disorganized because they feel they can talk their way out of anything. They are not detail oriented and can sometimes be unrealistic in their approach to solving problems. Influential people fear the loss of social approval and crave acceptance. Under pressure they will attack emotionally but not in public.

S stands for steady. These are slower paced, sociable people who are easy going, patient, calm, and stable. They're like the super-volunteers, following the leader and doing what they're told to accomplish a task. Coming up with innovative ideas or changing things is not their style. They can be indecisive, overly accommodating, passive, and sensitive, yet they are good listeners, empathic, and give reliable feedback. Steady people fear change and give in under pressure, complying with others demands, fearing they will hurt the relationship. They enjoy the status quo and need time to adjust to change.

C stands for conscientious. These are also slower paced people who are more task oriented. They like to be accurately detail oriented placing attention on high standards. Often they can be overly critical, sarcastic, and perfectionistic. Conscientious people are keen observers with an innovative, creative bent, yet they fear criticism of their work. Under pressure conscientious people avoid conflict, withdraw, and even plan strategies to get even. They are reluctant to make quick decisions and need a lot of information before they will do so. They need time to do quality work and time to analyze before making major decisions.

Knowing the behavioral style of others is a key to better communication and interpersonal effectiveness. When I know someone is only interested in the bottom line, a sensitive person would not approach him with long-winded chatter and stories. If you're communicating with a conscientious person, be ready with facts, figures, and details if you want their input. Very outgoing people often skip the details, so it would be wise to employ someone to take care of the details and let the influential person go out and talk.

DBT skill: Give—Keeping the Relationship

People who are passive and have difficulty asserting themselves often feel that, if they are too demanding and aggressive, it will ruin the relationship. To help a person become more assertive and feel comfortable, use the GIVE skill. It may seem counterintuitive but some people will respect us more when we speak up for ourselves instead of constantly giving in to what other people want:

> **Be Gentle:** Begin speaking in a positive voice. Be gentle approaching a topic. When you are engaging someone in conversation or you are being engaged, do not attack, call someone names, come off offensive/defensive.
>
> **Act Interested:** Show interest in what the other person is saying by nodding your head, matching and mirroring their actions, acknowledge your agreement, and do not distract yourself or interrupt them. Give them your undivided attention. Actively listen.
>
> **Validate:** Validate their point of view. Show them you are trying to understand their position. Validate their emotions by saying things such as: "I understand how you feel."
>
> **Use an Easy Manner:** Lighten up the situation with humor, take it easy, relax, and don't take yourself or the other person so seriously (adapted from Linehan, 1993).

GIVE DBT Skill Experientially

Divide the group members into As and Bs. Instruct them that the As will be telling Bs a 3-minute story about a vacation or something interesting they would like to talk about. Tell them to find a partner and face each other. Ask the Bs ONLY to step out of the room with you. Instruct the Bs to *actively* listen to As story by making eye contact, matching how the other person is sitting, subtly matching their hand gestures, nodding, and showing interest in what the other person is saying by asking questions. Return the Bs to the room and have the As begin their story. Do not process yet.

Next, tell the group that the Bs will this time be telling the As a 3-minute story facing each other. Keep the dyads the same group members. Ask the As ONLY to step out of the room with you. Instruct the As to act distracted, looking out the window, fidgeting with a pen or some object, reading a book. Tell them not to make eye contact, match the other person, or ask questions.

Return the As to the group, facing their partner, and have the Bs begin their story. At the end of the laughter, process with the group the differences in the two reactions and how it felt being on both sides, the storyteller and the listener.

Closing: Paper Tower Exercise

Divide up the group into smaller groups of four. Give each group an equal amount of blank, white, 8½ × 11 paper. Tell the groups they are having a contest to see who can build the tallest tower out of paper in 5 minutes. No tape or glue is allowed. Make sure the groups are ready and set the timer for 5 minutes and begin. As you get to 2 minutes, announce the time, and again at 1 minute, 30 seconds, 10 seconds and, finally, TIME'S UP. The group with the tallest tower still standing wins. You may want to prepare something as a giveaway before group, like pieces of candy or chocolate.

Inevitably, one group will have built the tallest tower, but it will fall in the middle of the exercise and they will have to scramble to catch up.

The purpose of this exercise is to explore the behavior styles of the participants. Having four in a group leaves the door open for having one of each of the four styles. Explore the following questions with each group:

1. Did you plan what you were going to do beforehand or did you jump right in?
2. Who was the leader of the group? How do you know?
3. Who sat back and waited for instructions?
4. Who gave advice on how to strengthen the structure?
5. Who took care of the details?
6. How did you work together as a team?
7. What did you learn about people from this exercise?
8. What did you learn about behavior from this exercise?
9. What did you learn about yourself from this exercise?
10. How would you have improved your structure?

16 Somatic Experiential Therapy

Warm Up: The Body Love–Hate Relationship

Clients often have a love–hate relationship with their bodies. This exercise allows clients to get in touch with feelings, attitudes, and beliefs about their bodies. Clients are invited to a body image party where they show up as the body part they dislike or seemed overly focused on. For example, one person might be "thunder thighs," or bulging belly, big nose, tiny butt, thin lips, etc. They introduce themselves within the group as these body parts and interact with the group. Process after 5 minutes.

Somatic Experiential[SM]

[Contributed by Michelle Rappaport, MA, LPC, NCC, CSAT-S Experiential Healing Center, Memphis, TN; http://ehcmemphis.com.]

SomEx[SM] is a Somatic Experiential Therapy modality used to treat trauma and addiction, and was developed by Kent Fisher and Michelle Rappaport, two experienced clinicians in experiential work with trauma and addiction. It uses the best of both worlds. It is the combination of the use of roles and props along with a body-centered attention to sensation and the autonomic nervous system.

This modality is very effective in treating addicts and especially those with shock or attachment trauma. For trauma survivors and addicts, the process of getting in touch with their bodies is quite a challenge. Therefore, the use of roles and props allows the individual to process issues that would be too "dysregulating," with space, by first taking it outside the body. Two of the most important pieces to focus on with participants are *resourcing* and using *somatic empathy*, with the therapist as a vehicle of change. Resourcing is a way to regulate the dysregulated nervous system. This is where experiential techniques including props, roles, art, and music are very effective. For those participants who have been numb or dissociated from their bodies using experiential techniques to amplify a resource is very effective. Embodiment, for those highly traumatized, is too activating and can lead to flooding, relapse, dissociation, or collapse. Therefore, beginning with a pleasant emotion is a safer way to start the process of healing. Ask clients: "How did you make it through?" or "What brings you a sense of connection?" These are examples of ways to begin the exploration into the resources of another. The next step would be moving into a prop/role to represent that resource and then explore bodily sensation even further.

The real transformation and renegotiation of trauma patterns happens in the oscillation (moving back and forth) between states of activation and resource while staying embodied and connected. Much of experiential work can be highly dysregulating and activating for the participant, which results in trauma repetition of high states of arousal in the nervous system that are ultimately dissociated. These cathartic moments might "feel good" in the short term but they don't have lasting transformation. SomEx[SM] moves slowly into these cathartic experiences while keeping the individual well resourced and connected to other people. SomEx[SM] works for discharge of activation in the body to a sense of completion. These experiences are all right hemisphere processing, and this is direct access to trauma that has been stuck in the body.

SomEx^{SM} in Practice

Imagery is one of the most effective props for use in a group or individually. Print pleasurable images on paper or find a page from a magazine and place them in proximity around the room. Begin with finding an image that is pleasurable, or they are drawn to in a pleasant way. The practitioner begins to SLOWLY explore the sensations in the body, amplifying movements, gestures, and attention. After the participant can embody the pleasant sensation, you can stop here or move to an image that brings up activation like a past traumatic event. Going slowly, begin to explore the bodily sensations associated with the traumatic event. Before the participant reaches high levels of arousal, return to the resourced picture. Repeat this process until the participant reports a change in the experience around the activating picture.

This process is the oscillation that renegotiates the neurological pathways of trauma. Due to the mirror experience that occurs in the group process, you can move into having group members mirror back their own somatic empathetic experience.

There are many variations on this exercise that can be done with other props, roles, sounds etc. The most important variation on traditional Experiential Therapy is the close attention and attunement to the body. In SomEx^{SM} we listen to the story the body has to tell. Using *somatic inquiry* while using the props, images or roles keeps the focus off the cognitive narrative and keeps the attention on the body.

After the exercise, allow for reflection and processing.

DBT Skill: Describe

The DBT core mindfulness skill describe is part of a trio of skills that work together seamlessly to help a person put factual words to what they experience without being judgmental. This trio comprises observe, describe, and non-judgmental stance. The observe skill is discussed in Chapter 20 and non-judgmental stance is discussed in Chapter 18.

When a person describes something, use just the facts. Describe what you know and what you see, hear, or feel, and try not to leave anything out.

You can describe what you observe in terms of color, texture, smell, taste, or sound. A black pen with a silver tip would be described just so. When a person answers judgmentally, they might describe the pen as ugly, useless, smearing, hard to write with, etc.

One of the most useful ways to take advantage of this important skill is to be able to describe thoughts and feelings. Many people have trouble describing how they feel and simply tune out or act out obsessively to avoid putting words to their feelings. A person might say: "I'm having angry thoughts," or "I'm having sad thoughts." It's not your job to judge the thoughts but to figure out what might be causing the anger or sadness and use another skill to reduce the emotional turmoil. The trick to remember is a person does not have to *act on* her thoughts or feelings. They are just thoughts and feelings. Instead, simply observe them, describe them non-judgmentally and let them go from your mind, replacing them with a past, safe, positive experience.

The language used when describing something needs to conform to reality. It's easy to confuse reality when our mind distorts it. By describing without being judgmental, a person will be able to practice getting in touch with their reality, versus the sense of isolation, boredom and resentments that come from addictive personalities or traumatic incidents.

It is also important to use positive language when describing something like your thoughts, feelings, and beliefs. Saying things like "my life is in shambles," or "I'm feeling down and depressed today," reinforces the mood and it can end up being a self-fulfilling prophecy. Contrariwise, when a person speaks positively, it gives them a sense of hope and inspiration.

Describe Skill Experientially

Give each group member a Hershey's kiss. Tell them to follow your instructions before opening or eating it. Instruct them to slowly open the foil wrapping concentrating on the crackle of the foil. Have them place the chocolate in their mouth without chewing. Chocolate aficionados never chew chocolate, by the way. Tell them to swirl the kiss around with their tongue slowly, touching the roof of their mouth until it melts. Tell them to be mindful of the texture, taste, and smell of the chocolate and then to swallow it. Ask for volunteers to describe the experience.

Closing: Affirming the Body Experientially

Have each client share what would happen if the body part they hate or dislike were missing, for example: "If I had no lips it would be hard to smile, difficult to eat," etc.

Now have each person write three affirmations to the body part they want to disown: "My lips are healthy. They allow me to communicate with others with a smile. They allow me to pronounce words, so others can understand me."

17 Resilience

Warm Up: Resilience

Lay out three hula hoops with the following labels:

#1. Difficult time or event in childhood
#2. One person who showed up for you during that time
#3. Strength that you now own due to the life event

Have each client step into the hula hoop and share briefly.

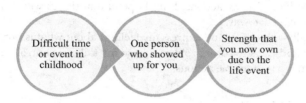

Figure 17.1 Resilience Hula Hoops

Resilience Factors

[Adapted from the International Resilience Project by Edith Brotberg.]

I HAVE external supports and resources like the people around me who love me unconditionally. And people who can set boundaries, so I will know when to stop. I have teachers and mentors to teach me how to do things and those who let me learn on my own. I have the support of people who help me when I'm ill.

I AM a person other people can like and love. I enjoy being helpful to others and empathize with them. I am respectful of myself and others and willing to take responsibility for my actions. I am hopeful that things will work out in a positive and effective way.

I CAN talk with others and express my feelings about what is bothering me. I creatively find ways to solve problems. I use my skills to control and manage my sometimes irresponsible actions.

How to Build Resilience

Ask the group to share experiences or childhood memories that were wonderful, beautiful, and loving from childhood. Have them explain these memories in visual, auditory, and feeling terms. What did you see, hear, and feel during these experiences?

Reframe and relabel the problem. It could be worse. Compare your situation with the devastation caused by an earthquake, flood, hurricane, or tornado. Situations can be seen for what was learned and gained, not only for what was lost.

Identify people you had strong bonds with, who helped you feel whole, accepted, and cared about. Identify your own resilience qualities that have enabled you to get up again, even though you may have fallen. Share goals you have today for your future and make specific plans on how to achieve them.

DBT Skill: Willingness over Willfulness

Are you causing your own suffering? Remember that pain plus non-acceptance equals suffering. When you are constantly fight reality saying, "it's hopeless," "this shouldn't have happened," or "I'm never going to amount to anything," you are only creating more suffering for yourself. When you don't accept reality, when you're not willing to participate in the world, you simply create more suffering. This is willfulness, denying life, trying to destroy it or simply ignore it by turning to drugs, self-harm, and eating binges instead.

Have you ever noticed that some people who experience adversity bounce back right away, and others keep the resentment and anger bottled up for years? Some people have a hard time dealing with negative emotions and they can't "just get over it." The people who bounce back face reality and are willing to participate fully in the world.

When you want to let go of your suffering, you have to radically accept the following:

1. Life's reality is what it is.
2. There is a cause to everything that happens.
3. We can create a life worth living and still have pain.

To solve a problem in your life you have four choices:

1. Change it
2. Fix it
3. Accept it the way it is
4. Stay miserable

What gets in the way of our acceptance is that we think if we accept what happened to us in our past, we are condoning it and saying it was OK. Actually, that is not the case. We cannot change the past and when we continue to hold on to it and not accept it as reality, we are allowing the perpetrators of our trauma to live rent free in our minds forever and ever. The point is not to forget and let go, moving forward working toward a life worth living.

The Willingness Walk

[Contributed by Susan Woodmansee MS, OTR, TEP, CAC 1, psychodramatist.]

The Willingness Walk can be done with one client alone or with three or four at the same time. Doing more than one adds some fun to the exercise but does rather blur the details.

Have each client write a list of what they are *not* willing to give up. Have them walk in a straight line to the other end of the room announcing the three things they will not give up with their hands extended out with clenched fists. Then have them turn around and announce the three things they *are* willing to give up and walk back to the original spot with hands open, palms facing up.

Closing: Purposes in the Pain

Hand out a sheet with "Purposes in the Pain." This is a visual reminder that their pain, hardship, and addiction have created greater purposes. Have each client circle the ones they connect with and can relate to the higher good.

Purposes in the Pain

1. It allows others to be there for us.
2. It allows one to find his or her own God-given destiny.
3. It allows for major life change.
4. It allows the opportunity for understanding and putting closure on "old" pain.
5. It allows one to get spiritually connected or reconnected.
6. It allows one to become grateful for simple things.
7. It allows one to get priorities in line.
8. It gives relief from repressed hurt and anger.

Process with each group member or divide group into smaller units and have them discuss among themselves.

18 Emotional Sobriety

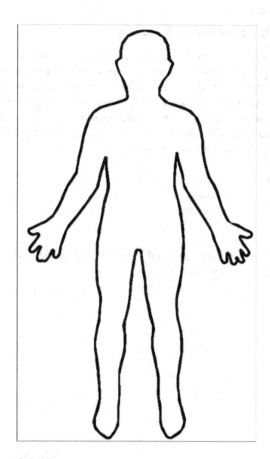

Figure 18.1 Emotional Sobriety

Warm Up: Emotional Sobriety

Hand out a simple body drawing (as in Figure 18.1) and ask clients to place the following feelings in the parts of the body where they feel these emotions. Have them use colored pencils or pens to highlight the emotions. Encourage them to think in terms of metaphors for their emotions: The brightness of the sun, the fierce redness of anger, a heart for joy, tears for sadness, etc. Avoid using words because this keeps them stuck in their logical mind and this exercise is to access the emotional mind through pictures:

Anger	Fear
Hurt	Guilt
Shame	Gratitude
Sadness	Joy

When each group member or client is finished, process what they have drawn and what they would like to share.

What Do I See in Others that Is Missing in Me?

Have participants stand in a square shaped formation. Hand each person a scarf and ask them to place it in front of them on the floor, creating a square shape. Ask each participant what positive characteristic, skill or ability they bring to the group. (For instance, I am a good listener, I have compassion, empathy, experience, leadership, sense of humor, a good education, etc.). When each person has shared why they chose what they did, ask each person in the group to move over to the person who has what they want more of. For example, if Joe has leadership qualities and I feel I would like to have some, I will walk over and stand by Joe. Each person selects another person who has what she wants and stands by him. Have each person process why they feel they have this need and what will move them closer to getting it.

DBT skill: Non-Judgmental Stance

As we've discussed already, there is a trio of skills made up of observe, describe, and non-judgment. It is impossible not to judge on some level. It's a lot like gossip. A person knows they will probably gossip and say something negative or derogatory this coming year. Yet, when he observes his thoughts he can ask himself: "Does this person really need to know this bit of juicy gossip?" Probably not. The same is true with judging ourselves and others. We have a choice to judge or not to judge and it all depends on remaining aware of the classic DBT question: "What helps me move closer to a life worth living?"

Let go of what is right or wrong, shoulds, could haves, and comparing ourselves to others. Judging and comparing are a person's worst enemies. None of us is a perfect creature; We all make mistakes. Give yourself a break and stop trying to be perfect in your eyes and in the eyes of others. When a person can express who he really is, he will find a way to be kind, to understand, and to be committed to a life worth living. This quest is what emotional sobriety is all about. Just because we are not abusing drugs or alcohol, sleeping around or gambling does not mean we are living an emotionally sober life. Being non-judgmental of ourselves and others is one key to unlock the mystery of working toward a life worth living.

In DBT, thinking we deserve to stay miserable, enshrouded in guilt and shame for our past actions, is irrelevant. Forgiveness is necessary to move forward in a new way. Ask yourself what holding on to your guilt and shame does for you. What benefit do you get from holding on to past traumas, abuse, and making irrational decisions? What has holding on to these things caused in your past? If it caused drinking, drugging, or other obsessive reactions, be honest about it.

Forgiveness is necessary to heal and to change the direction of our lives. Forgiveness does not mean acceptance. Forgive but do not *forget* and stop allowing the past to rent space in your brain any longer.

You will find yourself judging yourself and others from time to time. Simply turn your mind away from these judgmental thoughts and toward how you can use this interaction in a more positive way; perhaps giving the person the benefit of the doubt! Turn away from judgmental thinking and begin to focus on what is possible to achieve today.

Non-Judgmental Stance Exercise:
Drilling Down to Reach the Core Message

What is one thing that should be different in the world today? _____
_____

Why is that important to you? _____
_____

And why is that important? _____
_____

Drill down until you come up with your final answer, which may reflect a demand you are placing on reality: "Because I said so!" Realize that you are turning your own wishes into reality. Even if you have the best intentions, values, morals, and ethical teachings at your disposal, you are still interpreting reality the way you want it to appear. Unfortunately, per Marsha Linehan: "Reality as a whole does not work by our commands. Changing reality requires changing causes."

Give an example of when you were judgmental toward yourself. _____
_____

Give an example of when you were judgmental toward others. _____
_____

Give an example of when someone was judgmental of you. _____
_____

Notice and describe how each one of these examples makes you feel; judging yourself, others, and being judged.

Theme: Emotional Sobriety

Emotional sobriety is different from simply not using, drinking, sexing, gambling, or shopping excessively. Emotional sobriety is the goal we look forward to accomplishing so that we have no urges, cravings, or desires to want to continue to act out. Emotional sobriety is serenity in trusting that what is going on with me today is what is supposed to be happening, and when things turn emotionally unstable, I know how to reduce the emotional turmoil in healthier ways than acting out in my addiction. It's finding a way to regulate ourselves and maintain a middle path, balance approach to life. It's mastering the skills needed to balance our emotions and drives, our moods, eating habits, sexual drives, and sleep. In other words, self-regulation, through DBT, mindfulness, bodywork, and somatic experiencing, experientially, brings one to a sense of serenity and confidence in handling any situation, no matter how emotionally distressing.

The warning signs that we are relapsing into addictive thinking are as follows:

- Your inability to regulate strong negative emotions.
- Your inability to regulate your mood and behaviors.
- Your inability to regulate your use of substances and risky behaviors.
- Your inability to find longlasting, meaningful relationships.
- Your inability to roll with the punches.

What can you do about it? How do you get your life back in balance?

- Engage in deep trauma work to heal childhood wounds.
- Develop a strong support network of people who have been where you are now and have overcome their obstacles.
- Exercise, eat healthily, rest, and enjoy healthy pleasures including sex.
- Find meaning in work, hobbies, and passions. When you have a goal, working toward completing something you have a much better chance of achieving emotional sobriety. When you find your life's purpose and what brings you fulfillment you will know you are on the way to leading an emotional sober life.
- Process ups and downs when they happen instead of waiting days or weeks to deal with conflict.
- Develop inner resources to calm you down like, meditation, mindfulness, yoga, tai chi, and spiritual pursuits.
- When negative beliefs enter your mind, shaming you, ask yourself the following question: "What proof do you have that this statement is true?" "How does thinking this way benefit me in any way?"
- Make a list of other things you can do besides drinking or taking drugs.

Closing: A Letter From Your Addiction

Have them write a letter from their addiction to themselves, identifying what the disease has done to their lives, how it has caused emotional numbing and destroyed their ability to connect with themselves and others. Have clients share their letters by choosing another group member, facing him and have the other group member read the letter to the addict as the addiction. Let the addict answer the addiction and let the protagonist and auxiliary play out the scene.

19 Shame and Vulnerability

Warm Up: Natural Characteristics of a Child

Coordinate a play with each group member playing one of the parts below. You can add parts as you wish. Have each person come up with a 1- or 2-minute speech about why this characteristic is important to have, whether they had it, and if not what were the consequences of not being allowed to be a child growing up, instead having to grow up too fast:

1. Valuable
2. Vulnerable
3. Imperfect
4. Dependent
5. Needing
6. Immature
7. Wanting
8. Playful

Then have each group member BE the characteristic and meet other group members staying in their role pleading their case for why have this characteristic is so vital for their recovery. Have them switch partners a few times so they have an opportunity to explore different characteristics.

Shame and Vulnerability

> We are the most in-debt . . . obese . . . addicted and medicated adult cohort in
> U.S. history. The problem is – and I learned this from the research – that you
> cannot selectively numb emotion. You can't say, here's the bad stuff. Here's vul-
> nerability, here's grief, here's shame, here's fear, here's disappointment. I don't
> want to feel these. I'm going to have a couple of beers and a banana nut muffin.
>
> Brene Brown, Ph.D.

This quote from Brene Brown from her viral TED talk on vulnerability (see resources at the end of the chapter) explains why we have such a difficult time healing from trauma and addiction. We don't let our true selves be seen by others, so we put on a mask and act like a chameleon, giving in to everyone else's whims and desires, even when we want to say no. The only way to heal from shame is to talk about it, let it out so other people will know the truth and still not judge you unfavorably, because they've been there before. No one is perfect. We all have skeletons in our closet and when we accept the fact that we are still worthy of love and belonging *in spite of* our shortcomings, we begin to leave the past behind and look forward to a new future.

To be vulnerable means to let ourselves be seen, love with your whole heart, make a gratitude list, and don't take yourself or others so seriously. People who are genuine act with the courage to remain imperfect. They show compassion to others and cherish connection with themselves, other people as a member of humanity.

Vulnerability takes a willingness to say I'm sorry first. A willingness to act even though we don't know or cannot guarantee a positive outcome. A willingness to enter a new relationship without knowing if it will work out. The willingness to say no and accept when others say no to us.

We cannot selectively numb emotions according to Brene Brown. When we try to numb emotions like fear, anger, loneliness, and boredom, we also numb joy, happiness, and love. This numbing of our very beings happens when we make the uncertain certain, the opposite of what Dialectical Behavior Therapy teaches us. We numb when we can't live in the grey areas of life. Things have to be right or wrong, good or bad, weak or strong and, if they're not, we march our emotions to the extreme. We blame others, we strive to be perfect so we procrastinate and get nothing done and we pretend what we do has no effect on others.

Breaking Through Our Shame Defenses

There is a big difference between shame and guilt. Guilt occurs when someone does something against their values, beliefs, religious dogma, or societal norms. Shame is: "I am a bad person because of what I did, who I am, how I grew up or what I've not accomplished." Guilt is about the act, shame is a repudiation of the self. It is important for addicts and victims of trauma to look at their actions as guilt, not shame. According to DBT, you are doing the best you can and there is still room for improvement. You are much more than your addiction or trauma. It is only one part of your being. Your obligation is to find those other parts that make up your essence.

Unfortunately, we do not want to feel shame so we place it in a little box in our brain and say: "I'm over it." In actuality, shame lurks in the corners of our minds and speaks to us by constantly putting us down with words like "should," "must," "always," "never." Repeating the insults of the past, the "devil" inside us keeps our emotions at bay and we become too weak to answer shame back.

According to Ronald and Patricia Potter-Efron (1989), individuals who struggle with excessive shame often develop defenses that protect them from experiencing shame, including denial, withdrawal, rage, perfectionism, arrogance, exhibitionism, adaptation, and criticism. Here are some examples:

- Denial: I deny my uncle sexually abused me because there must be something wrong with me for him to treat me that way.
- Withdrawal: I withdraw from people out of fear of being shamed even more.
- Rage: I get mad at my wife so she doesn't get close enough to embarrass me in front of her friends.
- Perfectionism: Everything in my life has to be just right so other people won't think badly of me.
- Arrogance: I have to be the best so I don't have to be afraid of being the worst.
- Exhibitionism: I wear very low cut blouses to work and "come on" to all the married men.
- Adaptation: I am afraid to be different so I change like a chameleon depending on who I am with.
- Criticism: I criticize others about the faults I find in myself.

DBT skill: Reduce Vulnerability

All of us are vulnerable from time to time to triggers that cause us to crave and have urges for quick fix relief from emotional turmoil. Many people become more vulnerable when they are hungry, angry, lonely, or tired. When a person is in this frame of mind, his senses are dulled and his decision-making capabilities are altered. Then restless, irritable feelings follow, feelings of discontent, sometimes over a period of hours, days, even weeks, or months and we are on our way toward relapse.

The DBT skill of reduce vulnerability is a preventative emotion regulation skill that keeps us focused on positive feelings and behaviors, so we don't slip into hunger, anger, loneliness, or being tired. It is the actions we take daily to make our lives worth living and giving us the emotional strength to face adversity.

Reduce Vulnerability Worksheet

This graph in Table 19.1 represents the progression toward relapse that occurs slowly over a period of hours, days, weeks, or months. Identify what makes you vulnerable and place it in the first column under vulnerability. Circle the triggers that cause you to continue the slide toward relapse.

Table 19.1 Reduce Vulnerability Worksheet

Pre - Trigger	Trigger	Fantasy	Rituals	Acting Out	Feeling
Vulnerability	boredom				
	stress				
	hunger				
	anger				
	anxiety				
	tired				
	discontent				

Next identify the fantasy of engaging in this activity. What are you telling yourself will be pleasant if you engage in this activity? What negative emotions will you be eliminating and what positive benefits will you receive?

Next describe the progression of the ritual you go through after the thought of using or drinking. How do you prepare? What lies will you have tell to get out of the house and go to the dealer? What are the irrational thoughts you have during rituals that give you "permission" to act this way despite the consequences?

What do you do to act out? What is your drug of choice? How do you feel after you act out?

After you act out, how do you feel?

Closing: Resources on Shame and Vulnerability

Watch the following video with the group: https://www.ted.com/talks/brene_brown_on_ vulnerability.

Process with each group member what she gained from watching this video and what she will do differently now that she understands the connection between shame and vulnerability. You may want to show subsequent videos by Brene Brown on these subjects as you see fit.

20 Irrational Beliefs

Warm Up: Flexibility in Thinking

This exercise measures your flexibility in thinking, not your intelligence. Very few people solve more than half the first time through. However, they report getting answers long after the exercise has been put aside, especially when their mind is relaxed:

$$26 = L \text{ of the } A$$
$$7 = W \text{ of the } W$$
$$12 = S \text{ of the } Z$$
$$54 = C \text{ in a } D \text{ (with the Js)}$$
$$9 = P \text{ in the } S \text{ } S$$
$$88 = PK$$
$$13 = S \text{ on the } A \text{ } F$$
$$32 = D \text{ in which } W \text{ } F$$
$$18 = H \text{ in a } G \text{ } C$$
$$90 = D \text{ in a } R \text{ } A$$
$$200 = D \text{ for } P \text{ } G \text{ in } M$$
$$3 = BM \text{ (S.H.T.R.)}$$
$$4 = Q \text{ in a } G$$
$$24 = H \text{ in a } D$$
$$1 = W \text{ on a } U$$
$$57 = H \text{ } V$$
$$11 = P \text{ on a } F \text{ } T$$
$$1000 = W \text{ that a } P \text{ is } W$$

Answer Sheet for Flexibility in Thinking

  26 – letters in the alphabet
   7 – wonders of the world
  12 – signs of the zodiac
  54 – cards in a deck with the jokers
   9 – planets in the solar system
  88 – piano keys
  13 – stripes on the American flag
  32 – degrees at which water freezes
  18 – holes on a golf course
  90 – degrees in a right angle
200 – dollars for passing go in Monopoly
   3 – blind mice (see how they run)
   4 – quarts in a gallon
  24 – hours in a day
   1 – wheel on a unicycle
  57 – Heinz varieties
  11 – players on a football team
1000 – words that a picture is worth

Irrational Beliefs

When we begin to observe our thoughts and feelings, irrational beliefs flood our mind with unhelpful persuasion. It's like a devil sitting on our shoulder telling us what is wrong with us. We have to develop an angel on the other shoulder who can convincingly overpower the irrational beliefs. When you become aware of these thoughts, just observe them, then challenge them or distract yourself from the environment, to see things with a different frame of mind.

Some of the unhelpful thinking habits are:

Mental filter: A negative attitude filters out positive incoming messages that we reject.

Mind reading: Assuming you know what someone else is thinking (about us).

Prediction: The source of anxiety, thinking we can predict and control our future.

Shoulds and musts: Setting up unrealistic expectations of ourselves and when we don't achieve it, it's like a self-fulfilling prophecy.

Mountains and molehills: Blowing situations out of proportion by negatively minimizing the odds of how things will turn out.

Black and white thinking: Not living in the grey area of possibility. Thinking everything is either right or wrong, good or bad, living at the extreme ends of the spectrum.

Emotional reasoning: You assume the way you feel is reality; that you feel inadequate and that it's useless to do anything requiring effort.

Labeling: You label yourself a failure because of some of the mistakes you've made.

Personalization: Taking responsibility for what someone else has done or said. Like saying I'm sorry when you haven't done anything.

Dispelling Irrational Beliefs

IRRATIONAL BELIEF _____
If you could teach me how to believe that, how would you do it?

_____
IRRATIONAL BELIEF _____
How is this a problem for you? _____

_____
IRRATIONAL BELIEF_____
Who says? According to whom? Do you have proof that this is correct?

_____
IRRATIONAL BELIEF_____
What would you like to believe? _____
What's stopping you? _____
IRRATIONAL BELIEF – "I NEED TO BE IN CONTROL"
How will your family manage in future generations when you're not in
control? Were you born believing this? _____

_____
IRRATIONAL BELIEF – "I DON'T FEEL CONFIDENT DOING
THAT"
Therefore? _____
How does your lack of self-confidence mean {therefore}? _____

_____
IRRATIONAL BELIEF – "I CAN'T" _____
What would happen if you could/did? _____

I wish I Weren't So . . .

I wish I weren't so

_____

I wish I were more

_____

This makes me feel

_____

You can move this exercise into action by asking the client what they are willing to give up achieving what they want more of. Set up three chairs, two facing one, and have each client choose what they wish they weren't and have another group members sit on the chair facing the client. Then have another client play what they wish they were more and sit on the opposite chair. Now you have the client in the middle chair flanked by the two other group members. Have the two group members play their parts to sway the protagonist to their way of thinking.

For a more robust sculpt, choose another group member to play the feeling and act as a double for the protagonist saying things like: "That makes me feel_____ when you say it that way."

Emotional Mythology

[Contributed by Rebecca Walters, Hudson Valley Psychodrama Institute.]

To the group leader: Go to Appendix Seven and tear the paper in small strips with each emotional mythology. Put them in an envelope and pass them around to each group member at random. Have each group member read their sentence and engage group in discussion about whether this is true or not. Do not tell them these are myths before the exercise. This helps clients understand their emotions more clearly and there is nothing wrong with expressing them:

- There is a right way to feel in every situation
- Letting others know that I am feeling bad is a weakness
- Negative feelings are bad and destructive
- Being emotional means being out of control
- Emotions can just happen for no reason
- Some emotions are really stupid
- All painful emotions are a result of a bad attitude
- If others don't approve of my feelings, I obviously shouldn't feel the way I do
- Other people are the best judge of how I am feeling
- Painful emotions are not really important and should be ignored

DBT Skill: Observe

The observe skill is about focus. What we focus on in life is usually what we get. If we focus on nothing and waste our days engaged in frivolity or dangerous pursuits, we don't have much of a chance of achieving anything meaningful in our lives. If, however, we begin to observe the world, our thoughts and feelings and find meaning in things we have taken for granted, we will become more positive people.

We cannot choose to get rid of negative thoughts that cause us emotional pain. But we can choose to greatly decrease their power over us by choosing what we focus on. We can also increase joy, happiness, and peace of mind by turning our attention in a new way.

The observe skill is about noticing what we're feeling in the moment without trying to repress it. Simply observe that now you're having angry thoughts, sad thoughts, shameful thoughts without judging. Let go of the fact you have the right to be upset and turn your mind to something else less stressful.

Ask yourself, "How strongly do I want to feel relief and achieve peace of mind?" Observe your surroundings. Give yourself permission to just sit and observe the wonders of nature without focusing on anything else. Turn your mind toward what you are grateful for, a positively uplifting experience you enjoyed in the past, or something you can touch and feel that reminds you of warm, positive memories.

You are not pushing away emotional pain, you are simply observing that it is there, then making a conscious effort to focus your mind in another direction.

Closing: Let's Have a Party

Buy some cardboard party hats with chin straps. Place the following strips of paper on the head of each group member, one on each hat, without letting the group member see what is written on their head. Make sure to give the "ignore me" label to the most outgoing person in the group!

GEEK	IGNORE ME	LEADER
ASK ME	LAUGH AT ME	SMART
CREATIVE	PITY ME	FOLLOWER

Instruct the group to stand up and plan a birthday party together. Have them walk around the room talking to each person ACCORDING TO WHAT IS ON THAT PERSON'S HAT. In other words, they would ignore the person whose says ignore me (outgoing group members feel tortured when people ignore them). They would treat the geek as if he knows all the details, laugh at whatever advice that person gives, etc. This is a fun, yet powerful exercise in teaching people how to observe without judging others.

After everyone mingles, ask the group members to stand in a line across the room and ask each one what they think is on their hat. Most group members will answer correctly.

Process with the group what this exercise was all about. It's all about our preconceived notions about other people and how we judge them based on occupation, personality, and behavior. It's also a lesson in communication skills. Ask each member how they felt wearing their hat.

For an additional follow up, give each participant a marker and have them relabel their hat as to how they want to show up in their world. Have them share two or three behaviors that will be required if they stay true to their new label.

21 Codependency
The Root of Addiction

Warm Up: Boundaries

Where do you need to set boundaries in your life? Circle those that apply:

People
Mother Father   Son   Daughter   Spouse Brother Sister
Other _____

Places
_____
_____
_____

Things (circle all that apply)
Work   Relationships   Intimacy   Drugs   Alcohol Money
Privacy Time   Other_____ _____ _____

Boundaries Experientially

[Contributed by Marty Morrison, of blessed memory.]

Choose one boundary issue from the above list. For example, parents, money, relationships, physical, environment, intimacy, work, etc.

Choose someone (protagonist) who wants to explore how they need to set boundaries. Ask them what things or people are getting in the way of them setting boundaries, and then send them out of the room.

Assign roles to the different group members. Have them wear signs according to what the protagonist mentions as getting in the way and prep them on how to act within their role. Have the protagonist come back into the room. Place a sheet in the middle of the room with all the group members surrounding him and say, "This is your life!" "Where do you want these in your life?"

Theme: Codependency

Codependency is the root of addiction, caused by growing up in a dysfunctional, un-nurturing, strict, abusive family dynamic. We grow up conforming to our parent's needs, while our needs are not being met. Codependence is like being a child in an adult body, immature and frightened with low self-esteem, unable to set boundaries, and unable to flourish in your own reality.

Many clients come to treatment centers saying: "I don't know who I am." They have been active in self-defeating patterns of thinking, feeling, and behaving in an age-inappropriate way. As a result, according to Pia Mellody and Andrea Wells Miller (1989): "[P]eople who are codependent do not know how to relate functionally with themselves. When our caregivers are insecure, shaming and dysfunction, we assume this is normal behavior and we blame ourselves and continue this belief system as adults."

One of the most effective ways to treat codependency is with experiential therapy. Warning signs include loss of structure, indecision, procrastination, resentments, compulsively dangerous behaviors, defensiveness, depression, and self-pity. Cognitive Behavioral Therapy teaches the patient about the disease, breaking denial and delusions until they surrender to the disease process. According to Sharon Wegscheider-Cruse and her colleagues (1990): "[E]xperiential therapy is directed at the emotional pain of the patient, utilizing current and past history, genetic makeup, and personality to gain access to the actual process within the brain." In Experiential Therapy, we bring losses from the past into the present moment and deal with them in the here and now.

What creates long lasting healing from codependency is rebuilding our own sense of self within our relationships. It's about shedding the tears as we accept and forgive our past. It's learning the characteristics of the child and recapturing the inner child part of ourselves that is playful and vulnerable, learning to use our voice to be heard as we stick up for ourselves. It's about forgiving ourselves and others, not as approval, but as a way to move forward. It's about gratitude and finding it in all walks of life.

Devil and Angel

Arrange two empty chairs facing one another, one with angel written on it and one with devil written on it. Have each group member come up and sit in the devil's chair and share what he doesn't like about himself and how he talks to us with shameful comments. Then have him sit in the angel's chair and relate what he does like about himself and how he can talk back to the devil's shameful comments.

Process after a group member has sat in each chair, first process them sitting in the devil's chair, asking the group what they relate to and give feedback. After he sits in the angel's chair, process again.

DBT Skill: Objective Effectiveness (DEAR MAN)

The DBT skill of DEAR MAN is one of the interpersonal effectiveness skills to help people get their point across in a healthier manner, rather than being accusatory or losing their temper. DEAR MAN is an acronym which stands for:

Describe: Describe the current situation clearly to the other person. For example: When you *come home late and don't call to let me know.*

Express: Express how you feel using "I" statements. Example: "I feel angry." "I feel scared something's happened to you." "I feel disrespected."

Assert: Assert your wishes or state what you are asking for. Remember the difference between aggressive, assertive, and passive communication styles. For example: "And in the future I would appreciate it if you would call me and let me know you're going to be late."

Reinforce: Reinforce your wish by telling the other person the reasons behind the objective. Tell them *why* it is important. For example: "This is important because your dinner will be cold."

Be **M**indful: Stay mindful or what your objective is. Don't give in to excuses, rationalizations, or defensiveness.

Appear confident: The key word here is "appear." Make eye contact, sit up straight, speak clearly and forcefully without shouting or getting angry.

Negotiate: Be willing to negotiate. For example: "How can we resolve this issue of your not letting me know you will be late? If we cannot come to an agreement, I will stop making dinner for you."

Have clients review a recent scenario where they could have used DEAR MAN.

Messages Received From My Past

In my past I learned not to trust other people. These were the messages I received:

_____

In my past I was told or learned to ignore my feelings. These were the messages I received: _____

In my past I was told not talk to/about/when/where. Here are some examples:

_____

What I Believe in the Present

Today I don't trust people who _____

Because _____

Today I don't express my feelings because I _____

Today I don't talk about or admit _____

Because_____

Compare your answers and list the lessons you are still holding onto:

When it comes to not trusting I am still _____.

When it comes to not feeling emotions I still don't want to express them because

_____.

When it comes to not talking I still don't speak about_____.

22 Spirituality

Theme: Spirituality

> Many recovering people say, during abstinence, "I felt some kind of void inside me. I had no idea what that was all about. Now I know that was the empty space where my Higher Power belonged."

The Problem

Spirituality has different meanings to different people. Some people equate it with religion while others simply ignore it, spending their lives searching for meaning. Spirituality is the foundation, the answer, to moving from addiction and trauma to sobriety. Twelve-step programs, treatment centers, and outpatient facilities all promote spirituality as the pathway to change. After all, addiction is the antithesis, or the absence of spirituality.

Filling the Spiritual Emptiness

Indulgence in excess is a unique human experience. Animals know when to stop eating, drinking, and having sex. All they have are their physical urges and desires. Human beings, by way of contrast, have to struggle to find a balance in physical cravings because they also crave spiritual fulfillment as well. When this spiritual fulfillment goes unmet, humans become restless. Spiritual craving is harder to identify. People say they feel something is missing but they cannot identify what that "it" is.

Substances sometimes fill this void to produce a sense of instant gratification. Addictive thinking can lead people to attempt to quench this hunger for meaning with food, drugs, sex, or money. These objects give some gratification but they do nothing to solve the basic problem, which is <u>a</u> *feeling of satisfaction with life without constant longing for something different or more of the same.*

The Meaning of Spirituality

Why is it so easy to know what satisfies our physical needs and yet so difficult to identify our spiritual needs? The answer is that a human being is not just another animal based on intelligence. Humans are morally free beings and can choose whether to recognize their personal spirit and have a relationship with its source, or totally ignore it.

Human Characteristics

Human beings possess many other characteristics that make us different from other animals:

*   We have the capacity to learn from history and its consequences.
*   We can think about the purpose of our existence. Why are we here? What is our purpose for being on the earth? Why has our Creator seen fit to keep you alive in spite of your shortcomings and your attempts to destroy yourself?
*   We can think of ways to better ourselves and implement them.
*   We can delay gratification and think about the long-term consequences of our actions.
*   We have the capacity to make moral decisions, which may result in denying our bodies, behaviors it longs for.

    All of these capacities constitute the SPIRIT. This spirit is the part of us that distinguishes humans from other forms of life. When we exercise these unique human capacities, we are said to be *spiritual*.

What Does Spirituality Have to Do with Addiction?

Active addicts have not learned from the history of their past behavior that there are consequences to their actions, because they continue to drink, use, eat, act out sexually, gamble, or work obsessively. Their purpose in life is simply to get high and they seek no other purpose in life. They cannot seek self-improvement when their actions are self-destructive. Addicts cannot delay gratification and do not consider the consequences of their actions. Finally, addicts lack freedom, being dominated by their compulsions and obsessions.

A Question of Spirituality

Choose groups of three or four. Answer the following questions individually and then share with your small group members:

Discuss a moral decision you've made recently, what happened and how the decision has played out in your current lifestyle.

What have you learned from your past history?

What is the purpose of your existence on this earth?

Why are you here?

Why has your Creator seen fit to keep you alive in spite of your shortcomings?

What are three areas you feel you can better yourself? How will you implement these changes? When will you begin? Think beyond addiction.

What would happen if you delayed instant gratification and considered the long-term consequences of your actions?

DBT Skill: Improve

Sometimes we experience a situation that is not ideal. The DBT skill acronym IMPROVE is about improving a situation until it becomes more tolerable. What can a person do, now that he is in this stressful situation. The IMPROVE acronym stands for:

Imagery: Close your eyes and use your imagination to creative positive, healthy images of places you've been in where you've felt a sense of serenity, peace of mind, and happiness. Use all of your senses, see the sights, hear the sounds, feel the feelings you once felt, and relive this experience in your mind. This works because our subconscious mind does not know the difference if we're at home or at the beach, as long as we can visualize this type of happy or safe place. Go ahead, close your eyes, and do it now.

Meaning: Find what gives meaning to your life. What are you passionate about? Do things for others, volunteer, give back to the community. Create a short-term goal for yourself to complete a task and begin.

Prayer: "Psalms" is a good place to start. The author of "Psalms," King David, was a praying man. He was also someone who struggled in life, with temptations, enemies, and many battles. But his prayers of gratitude ("Psalms") were his path to peace.

Relaxation: Do something for YOU for a change. Take a stroll in the park, get a healthy massage, practice meditation, or take a nap. Do something every day to make your life less stressful.

One crisis at a time: Don't overwhelm yourself with all the problems you have for the next five years. Take the crisis you're in now and deal with it, accept it, or change it. There is a saying in my hometown in Arkansas: "Some people could complicate a one car funeral."

Vacation: Take a mini-vacation in your mind every day or a simple stroll around the block. Use your happy or safe place and spend a few minutes going on a vacation in your mind.

Encourage: Encourage yourself to deal with the stress in the ways we've discussed above. Keep talking back to that negative voice that tells you you're not good enough, those voices that put you down and tell you you're not good enough. Being grateful is the antidote for stress and negativity.

Closing: The Four Faces of GOD

Many people base their concept of GOD on their first impressions of how their parents related to them. If their parents were strict, they view GOD as strict because that's their first encounter with an authority figure. If there was not a healthy attachment as a child, the child grows up with a skewed impression of GOD. This sculpt helps the client choose the relationship with GOD that she wants in the present moment. This sculpt is adapted from the 1994 book by Sharon Wegscheider-Cruz, Kathy Higby, Ted Klonz, and Ann Rainey, entitled *Family Reconstruction: The Living Theater Model.*

Have four group members stand and face the larger group. Have the first person put their body in a position that would express a punishing attitude. Have the next person put their body in a position of being unapproachable. Have the third person put their body in a conditional position. Have the fourth person put their body in an unconditional stance.

The group leader asks the following questions:

Who in the group wants a relationship with a God who only punishes?
Who in the group wants a relationship with a God who is unapproachable?
Who in the group wants a conditional relationship with a God?

Research on the brain tells us when the mind is grateful, it floods the brain with oxytocin and it changes your feelings to ones of positive wellbeing.

Write down five things daily that you are grateful for, as you begin to develop a grateful state of mind. Train your mind to think differently as you lay down new neural pathways in the brain. Who in the group wants an *unconditional* relationship with a God?

23 Family Roles

Warm Up: Unconditional Love

Have clients introduce themselves from the position of someone who loves them unconditionally. For example, the person who loves me unconditionally is my wife. She would say: "[Group member] is strong, organized, and stubborn."

Have clients stand behind an empty chair in the role of the other. The role of the other is someone who loves unconditionally and share all the traits and wonderful things about the person in the chair, which is *you.*

Family Roles in Addiction and Trauma

The role a child plays in the family has a profound influence on the child as he or she grows up. According to the family dynamic, each child plays a different role in the structure. When a child suffers from an addiction or trauma, this affects the entire family, not just the addict or trauma victim.

Sharon Wegscheider-Cruse adapted family roles from Virginia Satir after her work with families and came up with the following family roles:

Hero: Usually the first-born child, the hero's job is to be able to make the family look good. They ignore the dysfunction in the family and put things in a positive light to others. The hero is usually a perfectionistic. Because many in the family are not emotionally unavailable, the hero steps up to the plate but inside feels fear, guilt, and shame. He ends up doing things for everyone else; it has to be perfect so people won't look at the family negatively, with a belief that if he does OK he'll *be* OK.

Scapegoat: In a family dynamic where an addict is present, the scapegoat will act out in front of others and rebel; anything to divert attention away from the addict and recovery. He is like the anti-hero, angry, resentful, hurt, and lonely.

Lost Child: The lost child is the silent one who wants nothing to do with the rest of the family. He stays out of the way and will not mention addiction or recovery. They do not like to create conflict. They feel as if they don't count; out of touch with who they really are. Inside, they have low self-esteem, feel hurt, angry, lonely, and inadequate.

Mascot: The role of the mascot is to be the family clown. While they bring humor into their role, they can also make inappropriate jokes about what's going on in this dysfunctional family, and this can hinder the recovery process. Mascots are insecure, thinking if they can make people laugh they will be liked. Underneath, they are embarrassed, angry, and shameful.

Addict: Others have added the addict as a role because addiction is a family disease and we're exploring how this role affects the family and the other roles within the family. The addict becomes the center of attention in the family dynamic. The world of the family centers on the addict. The other family members assume other roles to fill out the balance.

Group Exercise

Have group members identify the role they played in their family and how this role has continued into adulthood. Ask them who in their family they would like to approach about the role they played. When they select one or two family members, have them assign other group members to play these roles. Have them speak to the "family members" one at a time.

DBT Skill: Relationship Effectiveness (GIVE)

GIVE is one of the trio of the interpersonal effectiveness skills along with DEAR MAN, which is objective effectiveness, and FAST, which is self-respect effectiveness. GIVE stands for the following and is to be used to enhance relationships:

Be **G**entle: Effective communication cannot exist in a vacuum or with conflict. While conflict is normal, being gentle means to have a soothing demeanor, not lose your temper, and communicate your wants and needs while empathically supporting the other person by listening.

Act **I**nterested: Give the other person your undivided attention. Get rid of distractions and use active listening skills such as eye contact, head nodding, asking questions, and empathy.

Validate: Tell the other person how they have affected your life in a positive way. Give them sincere compliments about things they've done, without flattery.

Have an **E**asy manner: Relax and take it easy. Don't take things so seriously. Liven things up by using humor.

Give Experientially

[Contributed by Rebecca Walters, MS, LMHC, LCAT, TEP, Director, Hudson Valley Psychodrama Institute, http://hvpi.net.]

Pair up members of the group and have them face one another. You will give them four scenarios. Each member of the pair will play a role and a dialogue will follow. Encourage them to use the GIVE skill of being gentle, interested, validate and easy manner.

Scenario #1: One partner is the cop, one is the speeder. The speeder tries to convince the cop not to give him a ticket. Cop uses his GIVE skills and makes a decision based on these.

Scenario #2: One partner is a store owner, one is the employee. It's Christmas time and the store traffic is heavy. The employee wants to take a vacation during this period.

Scenario #3: One partner is a friend, the other a friend who just received a DUI. The friend with the DUI wants to know if his friend will let him drive his car.

Process after each scenario what happened, what decisions were made, and each how partner felt in his role. You can change partners for each scenario if you wish. Each group member should switch between the authority role and the submissive role to practice being in both situations.

Closing: Family Roles

End group by asking each participant to answer the following:

Where are you today from the group work we did today? _____

_____

Write your own progress note: _____

_____

_____

_____

Considering the role you played in your family, answer the following questions, for mother and father:

What I needed from you mom was_____

What I got from you mom was_____

What I needed from you dad was_____

_____

What I got from you dad was_____

_____

If the client seems ready, you can move into expanding what the client wants to say to each parent.

24 Healthy Intimacy and Sexuality

Warm Up: Your Lifestyle Inventory

This exercise was written by the late Dr. Richard D. Dobbins who gave me permission to use this many years ago in my couples' retreat.

Give out the Lifestyle Inventory below, which lists six abilities experts identify as important. Give yourself and your partner a score as follows:

1. Very little
2. Little
3. Some
4. Great
5. Very great

1. Supportiveness – The ability to give verbal and emotional support to your partner.
2. Independence – The capability, if necessary, to face live without your partner.
3. Interdependence – The need to experience verbal and physical support from your partner.
4. Spiritual desire – The ability to share quiet moments of reflection or prayer together.
5. Sensual desire – The experiencing of an intense need for touching, caressing, and kissing your partner.
6. Sexual desire – The experiencing of a deep need for sexual intimacy with your partner.

Score yourself and your partner and share the results with one another.

Table 24.1 Lifestyle Inventory: Partner One

Support	Independence	Interdependence	Spiritual	Sensual	Sexual
Very little					
Little					
Some					
Great					
Very great					

Table 24.2 Lifestyle Inventory: Partner Two

Support	Independence	Interdependence	Spiritual	Sensual	Sexual
Very little					
Little					
Some					
Great					
Very great					

Theme: Healthy Intimacy and Sexuality

The world we live in today is all about connection. Social media have become a booming, billion-dollar business; connecting old friends and classmates and giving people the opportunity to meet and engage with new people. Human beings are wired for connection and when there is not healthy attachment with a primary caregiver, people turn to anyone who shows them a little attention or affection, even a stranger. Or they turn to drugs and alcohol as a substitute for connection, so they don't risk the difficulties of an intimate relationship that is strong and lasting. Society today promotes promiscuity. According to Phillip Flores' work on addiction as an attachment disorder, "drugs are literally hijacking parts of the brain that nature put there so we could connect with other humans." It's everywhere, including offline and online media. Young people are being told that being with one person for life is limiting. "Go out my son and sow your oats," they are told, "and have sex with as many people as possible, so you'll be able to enjoy new experiences every day." Our children on their "smart" phones are only a few clicks away from the worst types of pornography, violence, torture, objectification of both men and women, and worlds of fantasy and distraction.

While this may seem enticing and exciting to young people, it ignores the fact that they are engaging in *intensity* rather than *intimacy*, and this destroys the bonds of connection that are lasting, meaningful, and fulfilling. Intimacy is all about safety and connectedness, causing the relationship to grow without being frightened, threatened, or upset. Connectedness is being in tune with the other person; common grounds of comfort being with one another and enough differences to keep things interesting.

The Eight Levels of Intimacy

Intimacy: In to me you see.

1. Physical attraction and a sense of something you like about this person.
2. Aesthetic intimacy is about general compatibility with common interests in music, arts, theatre, clothing, culture, and style.
3. Shared interests and hobbies. You love spending time together doing activities, games, movies, shopping, and other forms of recreation, for example. Primarily, you do not get upset when your partner spends time with other people or does things without you.
4. Intellectual intimacy is about having similar hopes, dreams, goals, opinions, and beliefs.
5. Spiritual intimacy is being on the same page of morality and ethics.
6. Emotional intimacy is having a best friend who you would call first when something happened to you. There is a feeling or security, trust, and safety.
7. Sexual intimacy is the physical act of sex including touching and foreplay mixed with romantic overtures. Intimacy is also the right to accept or decline sex without force, being made fun of, or coercion. And it's also about withholding sex as a tool of manipulation.
8. Unconditional love is loving someone no matter what someone does, says or is, you love them with all your heart and without expecting something in return.

In today's world, people meet at a bar and go from #1-attraction to #7-sex almost immediately, skipping steps 2–6. Then we wonder why there is a divorce rate of close to 70% or why we can't have a good relationship with anyone! Because people ignore the forms of intimacy that create long lasting relationships and focus on the intense feeling they get from having sex with hundreds of people, just because! Like alcohol and drugs, sex and love are also addictive when intensity takes the place of connection and attachment.

Questions to Develop Intimacy

1. What types of music are you interested in? Theatre? Art? Furniture? Clothing?
2. What would be your opinion if I spent time with some of my old college buddies?
3. What are your hopes and dreams for the future? What do you feel is your purpose in life? What would you ultimately like to accomplish in your lifetime?
4. What are your beliefs as far as morality and ethics?
5. What would it take for you to trust me? What would it take for you to feel secure and safe around me?
6. Sexually, what are some things you like and what are some things you are not willing to do? What's your opinion about our speaking or hanging out with ex-girlfriends or boyfriends? What are you comfortable with as far as my being on social media? What about pornography?

DBT Skill: Validate Someone Else

This skill is about repairing relationships and keeping meaningful connections intimate.

We all have a desire to be seen for who we truly are. When we have low self-esteem, we mask who we truly are for someone we think will fit in better with whoever we're talking to. The skill of validation is letting another person know that we appreciate the feedback and help we receive from them.

To validate someone effectively begin by saying how you relate to what she is going through; her struggles, feelings, and opinions. Tell the other person your own perspective on your relationship and how you understand her point of view. You don't have to agree with someone to understand her point of view.

Next, talk about who you think the other person really is. Be honest and accept her as she is. You can also let the person know what she's done for you that has improved your experience here and your life. Let the person know how important she is to you and how she's enriched your life.

Rephrase what she is saying in your own words, so she knows you're listening. Use good communication skills like making eye contact, nodding, and asking questions.

Go around the room and have each group member validate another group member or two. If one of the group members is discharging within the week, have everyone in the group validate him and his contribution to individuals and the group.

Closing: Healthy Intimacy Dialectical Dilemmas

On one end of the room call it "Very Much" and on the other end of the room call it "Very Little." Have group members stand and move along the line between very much and very little as you advance the following scenarios:

- I trust my own intuition when it comes to relationships.
- In relationships, I am more spontaneous rather than looking for a long-term commitment.
- I believe partners need to be similar emotionally to have a healthy relationship.
- I can fix my partner's problems as long as I am assertive and not aggressive.
- Honesty is very important toward building a long-term relationship but doesn't really matter if we're just going to hang out together.
- Sex is the most important part of our relationship.
- It's OK if I stay in an open relationship and not have to deal with the bad times.
- I have to know where my partner is at all times, who he is texting and speaking to, where he's been, what websites he visits, and who he speaks to at work.

25 Feel the Fear and Do It Anyway

Warm Up: Relationship Formula

Know I (So I can)
Know U (So U can)
Know Me

I have to know myself before I can know you and you have to know yourself before you can know me. Pair up group members and have them discuss the follow with one another. Process with the group at the end what they learned from this exercise:

To know me you would need to know that I _____.
For me to know you, what do I need to know? _____.

Theme: Feel the Fear and Do It Anyway

Fear has a way of making us prisoners in our own minds. When you can confront the fear by bringing it up to the person who is causing it, you have a much better chance of overcoming it. You have to know how to present your case. Assertiveness is a tricky skill. To some people, assertiveness or even being aggressive is a natural response to imminent conflict, or even petty disagreements. To passive people, it is very hard to muster up enough courage to feel the fear of speaking up for ourselves and do it anyway. It's hard to speak our minds on our own behalf. It is vital to learn the skill of assertiveness. Without it, your body becomes a storehouse of resentments and anger bound by the straitjacket of fear of confrontation.

However, when you confront this fear and push yourself gently out of your comfort zone, you will discover a harmony of spirit envelope you like a soft cloud. It protects you from your passivity while teaching you a lesson. That lesson is, feel the fear and do it anyway. Ninety-five percent of the time, you will feel better and get what you want in the end.

Another byproduct of feeling the fear and doing it anyway is that people will respect you more for speaking up for yourself. This seems counterintuitive, but it really works. People don't like other people who are wishy-washy and can't make up their mind about simple matters such as where to go to eat, what type of toothpaste to buy, or which movie you want to watch. When you stand up for what you want in a decisive way, you will gain the respect of the other person. In turn, they will begin to treat you differently, in a more positive way.

Some people have the conception that doing whatever we want without considering consequences is considered freedom. In truth, addiction is more like being a prisoner to the drug, alcohol, sex, person, food, gambling, etc. It's the farthest thing from being free to do whatever you want. True freedom means we have a choice in life and when we choose wisely, we attain a sense of freedom through that.

DBT Skill: Self-Respect Effectiveness (FAST)

The FAST DBT skill is part of the interpersonal effectiveness trio of skills. It is used when you feel your self-respect is being threatened when you are assertive with another person. When you use the FAST skill you will begin to feel a heightened self of self-worth and people will respect you more when you stick up for yourself. The FAST acronym stands for:

Fair: Be fair, respect other's boundaries and tell them how you feel.

No **A**pologies: Apologizing makes you look weaker, especially if it's about something you were not involved in. Saying "I'm sorry to have to tell you this BUT . . ." is a weak way of being assertive. In fact, it's not being assertive at all.

Sticking to your values: Stick to your values, beliefs, and moral teachings. Know what your values are and do not waver. Again, true friends will respect you when you respect your values and don't cross your own spiritual boundary.

Truth: Be truthful. Lying will just cause more problems later on.

DBT Fast Experientially

Place a strip of masking tape across the room with one side representing "I am successful with relationships," and the other "I feel like I'm always struggling with relationships." Have group members stand along the continuum based on their choice and ask each one why they are standing in that spot.

The Willingness Exercise

[Developed and contributed by Bill Coleman.]

[This exercise has been newly updated with additional material and can be found in the full-length book, *The Illustrated Guide to Psychodrama*, copyrighted, imprint 2017, published in early 2018. For further information, please visit http://www.cwcolemanbooks.com and or contact him by email at coleman15@mac.com.]

The purpose of this exercise is to evaluate the client's willingness to change a behavior, attitude, or belief he knows he needs to change. This exercise works best with a minimum of five group members. One serves as the protagonist and four serve as auxiliaries. Group members who are not playing a part are encouraged to offer feedback after the psychodrama is completed. Most group members, as they watch, will think about their own willingness dilemma and relate their experiences later.

I give a brief talk about my own journey, which has always been to discover if there is not some root feeling or belief or state of mind that drives all the others. Of course, this is a very big question . . . but, why not? I go on to state that I have come to believe there are two states that are "bedrock" and cannot be reduced to something more fundamental. The two are fear and shame. I also say that many will argue that this is an oversimplification. I acknowledge that but encourage the doubters to stay with me throughout the exercise.

I give a short didactic about shame and fear. I remind people that shame is not guilt and I clearly avoid any discussion of "toxic vs. healthy" shame. (Sorry Mr. Bradshaw.) I have an example of shame where I observed a young mother and her son in a supermarket. I make him to be about age 4. She is pushing a cart down an aisle and he is tagging along behind her. He starts to take things off the shelves and examines them as if he can read and understand the ingredients. Apparently satisfied, he puts the item on the floor. This is logical to him since he does not have a basket. What else is a 4-year-old to do? He repeats this on each side of the aisle three times. Eventually, Mom turns around and screams at him: "You little idiot, I wish you were never born." He freezes in his tracks . . . And this is a true story.

I ask the group what the boy will take from this. Everyone is mortified and agrees that he will think "I wish you were never born" will get etched into a neural pathway. I describe how this will get etched into a neural pathway in this brain as shame . . . forever . . . unless Mom immediately corrects herself. I also stress that all parents "lose" it. But not all kids are permanently damaged.

I follow this with a short discuss about neuroscience and neural pathways. Children have brains that were designed to learn, and learn they surely do. Abuse and trauma are the perpetrators of the pathway called shame. What follows this is a short description of what early shame develops into as the child matures. This can generate a lively argument about the effects of early shame.

On to fear. Here I offer a short talk on the amygdala, that it was formed in utero before the cerebral cortex. It is a basic survival mechanism that alerts the rest of the brain and body to the presence of a threat. Those threat alerts are fight, flight or freeze . . . and they are the same throughout the animal kingdom. And I remind everyone that we are all animals.

I give them an example. You are out walking and suddenly you hear a rattling sound near your foot. The amygdala says THREAT.

What do you do, instantly? Some will say scream or jump or run. I boldly correct that and say no, you freeze. You have no choice.

Then I offer thoughts about the "freeze" response and how it, too, like shame, becomes etched into the brain in the form of a neural pathway. All trauma causes this. If the traumas are repeated that freeze response is going to take a terrible toll on the development of the person.

This didactic sets up the psychodrama. But you have to be confident with the explanation and, if not, please get up to speed on your neuroscience.

Then we pick protagonist who wants to work on either fear or shame. Someone will come forward and sit in the front chair. The director proceeds with the interview. Let's call him Toby and he wants to work on fear. The interview doesn't change much if the choice is shame. Many say they have both and it becomes the director's choice.

After I get them to say, "I am Toby's fear," I ask a critical question: "Were you with him when he woke up this morning?" Then: "Did you go to breakfast with him?"

"What is your basic message to him at the start of his day?"

These questions are critical in setting the scene . . . being fear in Toby's head.

Setting the Scene

The director sets up three chairs in a row and a fourth chair in front. She stands behind the front chair, representing the behavior, attitude, or belief, and says to the group:

> In this chair there is something that represents something about you that you know you need to change. It could be a behavior, attitude, or belief; but you know deep down it needs to change.

The director pauses to allow the protagonist to think about it, then says:

> Would everyone please raise your hand. When you know what you might want to explore, please put your hand down. [This gets everyone involved in the question because they know why they are being asked.]

When most of the group members have lowered their hands, the director slides the chair in front of each group member and asks them what is in the chair for them. The director can then ask group members to describe their attitude, behavior, or belief, or choose someone from the group to be the protagonist.

In this scenario, a group member offers to be the protagonist and identifies her "chair" as shame or fear. The director interviews the protagonist in her role as shame.

(This may be the first time a group member has thought about identifying a part of herself as a ROLE to be played. The protagonist is identifying her role as shame. As the director, you want to make sure the protagonist responds in first person to concretize the ROLE.)

The director asks: "What are you?" The correct answer is "I am [name of protagonist]'s shame." The director may need to double this response until the protagonist gets used to answering as "shame." The director then asks a series of questions to "shame," continuing to make certain the protagonist continues to answer in her ROLE, not as herself:

- How long have you been in her [name of client]'s life?
- Where did you come from? Surely, she wasn't born with you?
- So, you're a big part of her life, aren't you?
- Were you around this morning for breakfast?
- Are you here now?
- What is your basic message to her at the start of her day?
- Tell me some of the things you tell her?
- What kind of allies do you work with? [Depression, anxiety, trauma, addiction, etc.]
- What do you do for her? Why does she keep you around? [This question really gets the client to think about her life and dilemma in a totally different way.]
- What's your kryptonite? What makes you weaker?

(We are literally trying to separate the role from the protagonist, so make sure you reframe the question to be directed toward the ROLE, not the person.)

The director then turns to the group and asks them if anyone has any questions for the ROLE.

This is crucial to the exercise since it involves other group members and they will ask questions to the ROLE. Intervene if necessary to make sure the question is directed to the ROLE, not the protagonist. Make sure the ROLE stays in the here and now and does not go deeply into her past. You are attempting to establish what defense mechanisms the protagonist uses.

After the role is established and the group has had an opportunity to ask questions, the director asks the protagonist to stand next to her and chose someone in the group to play this ROLE (shame).

The director asks the person now playing the role of shame the same series of questions.

The director checks in with the protagonist to make sure the answers are correct. You may have to prompt the auxiliary playing shame to answer exactly as the protagonist did previously.

The director now turns to the protagonist standing next to him and asks her to fill in the following sentences:

I am not willing to give up my shame because_____.

> Choose someone in the group to repeat that and have them sit in the row of chairs on the right.

I may be willing to give up my shame if _____.

> Choose someone in the group to repeat that and have them sit in the row of chairs in the middle.

I am definitely willing to give up my shame because _____.

> Choose group member to repeat that and have them sit in the row of chairs on the left.

Now, bring the protagonist behind the three chairs and have each person repeat their line. Now ask the protagonist: "On a scale of not willing to definitely willing, where are you right now?"

Wherever the protagonist says, have him go to that position in the line and explain to them why he is at that point and what it is going to take to get to the "definitely willing." As he is explaining this, have the person playing shame in the single chair turn around and tell the protagonist: "I'm still here." This creates a tension between what the client says he wants and the negative voice of shame. Tell the protagonist that this is going to be an ongoing conflict and if he wants to get rid of shame he is going to have to get some help.

Have him choose someone in the group to be a friend or sponsor. Have the protagonist tell the friend what he would like the friend to tell him when he calls for help. Develop a "cheer" between them like "you can do this," or "to hell with shame," and have the group yell it out for the protagonist to hear.

26 Inner Child Rescue

Warm Up: Inner Child Work

Client chooses someone in the group to be their inner child.

Have the client describe three characteristics of her inner child at a young age (fearful, fun loving, and innocent).

The client then chooses group members to represent each family member in her sculpt. Have her describe briefly each member and put them in the room according to the distance or closeness of their relationship to the child. The client steps into the role as the protagonist and inner child. Allow the protagonist to say one or two sentences to each family member and role reverse if needed.

At the end of the sculpt have a group member scribe the answers to the following question: What messages did this child receive growing up in this home? This is opened up to everyone for input.

You can also ask what behaviors might be showing up in her adult world today.

Theatre of the Mind: Inner Child Concepts

Explore with the group the messages and rules they received as a child, either verbally or rules and messages they assumed, based on family dynamics. See if your group can come up with some of the following inner child concepts and possible behaviors:

Message	Possible behavior
"You're stupid"	No motivation or work too much
"Don't cry"	Don't show feelings, be positive
"You're nothing but trouble"	Argumentative or perfectionistic
"My best little boy [or girl]"	I have to please everyone
"Something bad is going to happen"	Negative, critical, cautious, anxious
"Family comes first"	Lack of intimacy, family enmeshment, guilt
"Work first, play later"	Stay busy, work too much, few emotions
"It's not OK to touch or hug"	Sexual inhibitions or acting out, touch starved.

Inner Child Guided Meditation

Find a space in the room where you can get comfortable. It helps to shut your eyes to go inward and get quiet and still. Begin to breathe deeply, imagining you are breathing in clean white energy, allowing your breath to slow as you inhale, imaging the white light bringing peace as you go to a place that feels safe for you. It may be in a forest, a beach, or that special place you have been to before, or a place in your imagination that allows you to connect with your breath. As your body relaxes, you hear sounds of laughter as you become aware of children playing nearby and you notice one in particular to whom you are drawn by his energy and you realize it is your inner child. You remember what he looked like but it has been a long time since you have connected. He runs up to you with excitement as his words tumble out as he talks to you. You listen intently as you kneel down to his level. His words are impactful. You hear the other children laughing as they return and suddenly your inner child is running and playing with the children. You stand up and slowly return to your safe place, being aware of the words your inner child spoke so clearly to you.

Taking a few deeper breaths, you return to the room and to your adult self.

Inner Child Circle

Give out three 3 × 5 cards to each group member and a dark marker.

Have each group member put each family message on a card. With masking tape, make a circle in the center of the floor. Have each group member take a blank card and draw a symbol of himself as a baby and put his name on it. Put in the middle of the circle. Have group sit around the circle and ask: "What messages *should* this baby have heard?" ("I want you"; "You're beautiful"; "I like the way you did that"; "It's OK to cry, and so on".)

Draw a bigger circle around the first one. Put the family of origin messages in the larger circle. Ask each group member: "How do you feel about those messages as you read them now?" In the outer circle, put pillows around the circle. On different cards, have each group member write down her medicators that she *uses*, to *not feel* these messages and put them on the pillows:

> Imagine a three-dimensional dome. I invite you to get in touch with your inner child. How easy is it going to be?

We can see better when we get connected to our inner child. But we cannot get to the inner child because of the medicators. Like recovery from heroin, detox, feels like the flu and a person feels like he or she wants to die. Unless you learn AND CHOOSE a different way, you'll continue to use. Have compassion for yourself. You know how to have compassion for others in the room, share it with yourself.

DBT Skill: Burning Bridges

Willpower doesn't work in stopping addiction, you have to choose to stop and tell everyone you know you quit!

In the second edition of DBT skills training handouts (2015), Dr. Linehan introduces several new DBT skills specifically for addiction treatment. One of them is this skill called "Burning Bridges." Burning bridges is about getting rid of everything that makes addiction possible including throwing away paraphernalia, liquor and pill bottles, putting blocks on your computer, erasing dealers' phone numbers, and many more.

Use the radical acceptance skill and accept the fact that you have chosen abstinence over using. Make a list of everything you will throw away that could be a trigger for using again. Show the list to a sponsor or friend you can trust and tell everyone you know: "I'VE QUIT!"

Then begin to build new bridges. Remember, cravings and urges are linked to smells and visuals. Stay away from old images that used to trigger you and smells of alcohol or marijuana. Instead, substitute what you look for pleasant, invigorating images of success and accomplishment while concentrating on smelling new fragrances like coffee and lemon that remind you of fresh fruits and aromas of a new day!

Surf the urge when it happens. Remember, you don't have to act on a feeling or thought, let it go and wait for the urge to pass, like a wave in the ocean, eventually it will disappear.

Become more active in appreciating things in nature that you would normally take for granted. Watch things change, give yourself permission to just be with yourself, and be OK with it.

Key closing

Hand each client a key (keys are often available for free at any place that duplicates keys, where the mistakes are thrown away) and have her identify one key that will successfully open the door for her to move beyond the medicator to loving and protecting the inner child. Have each group member share the key to success.

27 Neuro-Linguistic Programming (NLP)

Introduction to NLP

In his book, *Using Your Brain – For a Change* (1985), Richard Bandler, founder of NLP along with John Grinder says: "People spend more time learning how to use a food processor than they do learning how to use their brains . . . You're stuck with your memories and told to be yourself – as if you had an alternative. You can learn to use your brain in more functional ways. That's what NLP is all about."

It's about how linguistics (language) can be used to change our neuro (brain). Instead of going into a lot of technical jargon, this chapter contains several exercises that will help you learn to program your own brain. In that sense, the theme of this chapter could be "CHANGING YOUR MIND." In a sense, these types of what we call NLP pattern can be used extensively throughout this book to enhance your experience and model excellence.

For example, we experience life in three ways: Visually, auditorily, and kinesthetically. In other words, what we see, hear, and feel. Your brain is full of memories, pleasant and unpleasant, which make you who you are. And you can change the intensity of any experience in either direction by simply expanding or contracting how you view, hear, or feel in that experience. Even a past experience can be changed so it does not have the intensity it once had. Flashbacks, dreams, and past experiences that continue to pop up in your mind can be wiped away using an NLP pattern called the "Swish Pattern."

Take a pleasant experience you once had and practice learning how to run your own brain. Change one of the following elements at a time, do not combine them, and notice how your experience changes:

- Vary the intensity of the color of the experience, moving from color to black and white.
- Change the distance, pushing it farther away and bringing it closer.
- Change the duration, taking your time to experience the color, sounds, and feelings of the experience.
- Change the clarity of the picture to fuzzy from clear.
- If there is movement, change the direction of the movement, slow it down, speed it up, see how that changes your experience.
- Notice any texture or pressure changes, skin temperature, anxiety, as you experience any of these submodalities (that's what they're called!).

Think about how you experience your past in your mind. You might view your positive experiences in black and white and your negative experiences in bright, living color. If so, no wonder you dwell on the negative experiences! What if you switched it around and next time you think of a negative experience, turn it into black and white, dim the color, lower the sound, and move the sensation in a different direction. Takes those positive experiences and blow them up on a movie screen in your mind, seeing bright vivid colors and beautiful sounds, as you feel the warmth and closeness in your mind.

Your Attitude Determines Your Altitude:
A Guided NLP Meditation

This meditation is a series of affirmations that can be converted into quotations and passed out to your group. Ask each client what the quote means to him. Or simply relax the group with deliberate breathing until they are fully relaxed and say the following pausing a few seconds at each ellipse (. . .):

Your attitude determines your altitude . . . Realize that to become a better listener, people don't care how much you know, but they know how much you care by the way you listen . . . Remember, you carry around the missing puzzle piece that makes others' lives more complete . . . and now come to realize that you have the ability to let your mind dwell on your strengths and that problems are just opportunities for you to improve . . . And I wonder how quickly you will ask yourself questions that will affirm these affirmations and how easy and natural it's going to be to repeat these to yourself each and every day . . . And how soon will you realize that attitude is just a state of mind, that your mind can only hold one thought at a time and how wonderful you will feel when you make that thought a positive one . . . Remember, you cannot help the way you feel, but you can help the way you act and think . . . I'm wondering who the next person is that you will give unconditional love to when you understand that you can love them into, NOT IF THEY CHANGE . . . Realize that life is a ball but you can't dance in the mud . . . Really know that you don't put your diamonds and your garbage in the same place in your home, so why do it in your mind? . . . So ask yourself, would I rather be right or happy?

Understand that what we dislike in others we dislike in ourselves, anyone who angers you, conquers you . . . and forgiveness is the fragrance of the flower that is trampled on . . . Know, really know, that to the degree you give others what they need, they will give you what you need . . . Because you are the captain of your own ship, you are the chef in your kitchen, you are the director of your own movie and you are the author of your own experience . . . So if it's meant to be, it's up to me . . . Just like a plant, you plant a seed in the ground and wait for it to grow. You don't go out every day and uproot the earth to see if it's growing. You unconsciously know it is and suddenly you go outside one day and there is a tiny shoot peeking out of the ground, a tiny sapling that will continue to grow and grow and grow, with water and positive sunshine, into a tall oak tree, full of vigor, vitality and life . . .

Because you are the ultimate gardener in your own garden and, finally, if you think you can or you think you cannot, YOU'RE RIGHT!

DBT Skill: Positive Reinforcement

The DBT skill of positive reinforcement is about finding positive things to do with your time. So many people with addiction and trauma wallow in self-pity, depression and anxiety that they lack the motivation to find something positive to do, rather than turn to drugs and alcohol to soothe their troubled souls. Actually, the key to emotional sobriety, and *staying* sober, is finding something in our lives we can look forward to completing and working toward that goal. Whether it's a job, owning your own business, a hobby, or volunteering, doing healthy activities for ourselves is what makes our lives meaningful and filled with purpose.

Another element of this skill is to get in the habit of giving other people positive reinforcement when they do something kind and considerate to you or others. When you get in the habit of finding the positive in others, you will automatically become a more positive person yourself:

What are some short-term positive experiences you can look forward to doing?

_____

_____

_____

What are some long-term positive experiences you can look forward to doing?

_____

_____

_____

List a number of activities that you might enjoy doing for yourself that are positive:

_____

_____

_____

Decision and Learning Strategy Elicitation

> There are no unrealistic goals, just unrealistic time frames.

What gets in the way of our learning a new way to live, a new skill or a new behavior?

1. **Perfectionism:** People believe that they must understand everything the first time they are exposed to it. If they don't understand immediately, they feel incompetent and negative about the learning experience.
2. **Unproductive comparisons:** People believe they are to be as good as their mentor, teacher, or sponsor immediately. Again, this is a time frame problem and a perfectionistic problem. People make comparisons between their current abilities and the expert or ideal self.

Convincer Strategy Problems

Why do we refuse to be convinced sobriety or happiness is for our own good?:

1. We have no external evidence about our skills without someone outside evaluating us or giving us verified results.
2. We may never be convinced that we understand a topic fully or have become skilled enough even though we are competent in other people's eyes.
3. We are constantly seeking to know "everything" before taking action. We are convinced we will never know enough to act on it.

The truth is that all decisions are based on incomplete information!

Let's Play Therapist

Have two group members face one another. One asks the other the following questions. These sets of questions can be used for addiction or other co-occurring mental health issues.

Addiction to Alcohol or Drugs, Sex, Gambling, Food, Shopping, etc.

What happens when you get the feeling you want to drink or use drugs OR [other addictive behaviors]?

> What's important to you about continuing to _____?
> What's important to you about [their answer]?
> What's important to you about [their answer]?
> How does it make your day different when it happens?
> How did you arrive at this understanding?
> How do you know you are an alcoholic or drug abuser or have an addiction to _____?
> What lets you know you have an addiction rather than something you can control socially?
> What other meanings can you give this behavior in terms of benefit to you? What other meanings have others given it?
> What's important to you about staying sober? What's important to you about [their answer]?
> What's important to you about [their answer]?
> Are there pieces of that already happening?
> How will your life be different when you are sober?
> How do you think your life will be when you overcome your addiction?
> What do you need to do now to keep the changes going?
> On a scale of 1–10, where are you?
> How will you do things differently when you have more serenity and peace of mind?

Depression/Anxiety

> Does feeling depressed equal depressing yourself?
> What is the benefit to you continuing to stay depressed and anxious?
> What's important to you about that?
> What's important to you about [their answer]?
> What else affects your mood?
> How do you know you're slipping into depression or getting anxious?
> How do you stop yourself?
> What stops you from being happier?
> What are you like when you're at your best?

How will you feel when depression (anxiety) is no longer an issue?

What other meanings can you give to this behavior? If you could see it another way, what would have instead?

What's important to you about [their answer]?

What's important to you about [their answer]?

What's important to you about being happy?

About being calm?

What's important to you about [their answer]?

What's important to you about [their answer]?

Are there pieces of that already happening?

How will your life be different when you are happy?

How do you think your life will be when you live a life of happiness?

What do you need to do now to keep the changes going?

On a scale of 1–10, where are you?

How will you do things differently when you have more happiness, calmness and serenity?

Closing: Your Ideal Life

Describe one scene in your life when you felt content, successful, accomplished, proud, and at peace. Have one person stand and imagine he is seeing himself on a movie screen as he describes in detail what he is wearing, where he is, who is around him, what he is doing and how he feels. Give each person at least 5 minutes to describe in detail this special event. This could open up discussion for what is important to the client, and some ideas how to incorporate these into his present life.

28 Building Trust for the Future

The Trust Diagram

	COMES MOST EASILY	NEEDS MORE ENERGY

Be Reliable:

Do what I say I'm going to do when I say I'm going to do it.

Be Open to Feedback:

Willingness to give and receive feedback and share Information.

Radical Acceptance:

Radical Acceptance and Non judgment even when we don't accept their behavior.

Be Congruent:

Walk my walk, talk my talk and practice what I preach.

Harmony is important. I might go along even if I don't believe (sometimes)

	KNOWN TO SELF	NOT KNOWN TO SELF
KNOWN TO OTHERS	**OPEN** What I know I know Explicit knowledge (Documented and stored knowledge)	**BLIND** What I know I don't know Knowledge gap (Documented and stored knowledge)
NOT KNOWN TO OTHERS	**HIDDEN** What I don't know but others do know Tacit knowledge (Knowledge in the minds of others)	**UNKNOWN** What I don't know I don't know Unknown knowledge

Figure 28.1 How to Build the Trust Back

Theme: Trust

The trust diagram in Figure 28.1 represents the four elements of trust needed to sustain and maintain a long-term relationship. For people with addictions, these elements are necessary to rebuild the trust with family members and spouses. After years of hiding and lying to cover up addictive habits, you need to be reliable by doing what you say you're going to do when you say you're going to do it. There needs to be openness in the relationship, where a person is willing to accept feedback and share personal information with those they care about. Just like the addict wants everyone to accept him for who he is, most relatives and friends do not understand addiction. Therefore, radically accepting others even when we don't agree with their behavior is a first step in having people accept you for who you are. Radical acceptance and nonjudgment of others will help people with addictions change the way they act toward others and others will reciprocate. Finally, a person needs to be who they say they are, instead of wearing a mask and changing it with each person they meet. Recovery demands that we become more vulnerable and let people see our true selves, with all the warts and foibles we've experienced. When a person can walk the walk and talk the talk, practicing what he preaches, he sends a clear message that he can finally be trusted for who he is and relationships begin to change for the better.

The Johari window (lower illustration), was developed by Joseph Luft and Harry Ingham in 1955. Mental health professionals, coaches, and business consultants have used the Johari window for team building and personality development. Recently is has been adapted to help people with addictions and trauma to understand themselves better and uncover how they come across to other people and their perceptions of other people as far as what they are hiding inside.

The Johari Window explores what we know that others know and what we know that others don't know. It also explores what we don't know that others know about us and what we and others don't know. The goal of the Johari window is to discover what we don't know, that others know by open communication and exploration of self as we step into that space what we don't know about ourselves as we challenge ourselves to get out of our comfort zone and make the window pane of being as open as possible so we both know.

Trust Exercises

Using the two illustrations above fill in the quadrants for what you need to do to build back the trust with your loved ones by examining each of the four elements and figuring out how you will incorporate that into your recovery plan.

Use the Johari window to explain what you know that others know and what you don't know that others know, according to the four quadrants. This exercise in openness toward yourself and others will help you understand what specific actions and behaviors you need to reveal to loved ones to build back their trust in you.

DBT Skill: STOP

The STOP skill is a simple way to stop thoughts, feelings and stimuli from becoming stressful events. As the quote above says, in the space in between the stimulus that triggers people and the behavior people often take emotionally lies the freedom of sobriety, less stress, and a more fulfilling life.

S stands for STOP. When a person is stimulated to want to drink or use, get angry or say something you will regret later, STOP for a moment, stand back and think about the consequences of past actions.

T stands for TAKE A DEEP BREATH.

O stands for OBSERVE. Identify what the person is feeling or thinking and remember, it's just a thought or feeling; you don't have to act on it impulsively. Simply observe and let it go like an egg flying off a slick frying pan.

P stands for PULL back/put the situation in PERSPECTIVE. Think about the bigger picture in term of consequences of acting impulsively. Is there something else a person can do to distract himself and get his mind off the trigger?

Talk back to that negative voice in your mind telling you one more time won't hurt anything. Say STOP to answer back the negative voice and make it a positive forceful voice inside your head.

Closing: The Trust Exercise

Find a team mate and one person stand behind the other. The person in front is blindfolded and the task of the team mate is to lead the person around a number of obstacles without hitting anything and keeping the blindfolded person safe. This exercise should last about 5 minutes. If suitable space is available, one can do this exercise outside. Once finished the couple process this exercise. If time permits, you can reverse roles, so both experience being lead and leading.

29 Bodywork

Warm Up: Bodywork Movement Circle

[Contributed by Steve Sommers LMFT LMT, Certified SomEx® Practitioner and Supervisor, Authorized Senior Instructor of Jin Shin Do® Bodymind Acupressure®; Private Practice in Brentwood TN; www.Bodyperspectives.com; Bodyperspectives@comcast.net.]

A group movement circle is most useful at the beginning of a session, but can certainly be used at any time during a group process. Group movement at the beginning of a session creates more permission and safety for movement to be used as individual group members star in their own experiential/somatic/psychodramatic pieces later in a session.

Process

The practitioner chooses a song 3–5 minutes in length. The group stands in a circle, arm's length apart, if space permits. The practitioner instructs the group to listen to the music. The practitioner states that all movements, big or small, fast or slow, in rhythm to the music or not, danceable or not, are welcome. The first person who feels a particular movement starts to move in a repeated pattern. Then all the group members join that person in the pattern until there is a space of approximately 15 seconds of everyone doing that pattern of movement together. Then the next person around the circle changes the movement into anything they would like – related to the original movement in some way, or not. The group all does the same movement with the second person. The process goes around the circle until the song ends. The practitioner then leads the group in a short, guided awareness, encouraging participants to notice what is happening inside their bodies after these playful group movements. Finally, there is a request that each group member shares her awareness of her body through the experience and in the present moment. Often there is deeper awareness of pleasurable, open, alive sensations in the body. Sometimes, there is also awareness of stuck or uncomfortable sensations in the body. This shift from experience to thought and expression is in line with the goal of clients modulating between body sensations and thoughts, feelings and experiences to reach a point of calm.

Additionally, it is vital to provide trauma survivors with positive experiences of present body awareness because there is often unpleasant or intolerable internal awareness that leads to disassociation or compulsivity/obsession. As the somatic practitioners say: "Resource, resource, resource." Eventually, all trauma survivors need internal body anchored resources to lean into as part of the healing process.

Group movement is just one way to reach this goal. But, there are many others!!

Bodywork and Embodiment

[Contributed by Steve Sommers LMFT LMT.]

One of my favorite definitions for trauma is: "Anything that goes beyond a person's ability to regulate (or be resilient) utilizing his/her normal coping skills." When we lose our feelings of safety, and our level of normal coping is breached, the human body goes into life-saving mode (disregulation, fight/flight/freeze, shock, obsession or worry, deep grief, etc.)

All life-saving modes are designed to return a person to safety. If there is not a return of true safety, there is a restriction or limitation in embodiment. Some of the most common forms of restriction in embodiment are retreating into the thinking brain, disassociation, numbing out of body awareness, and chronic muscular and connective tissue tension patterns. All these forms of trauma response can be renegotiated through bodywork and embodiment techniques.

In addition to creating positive body anchored resources, here are some other common benefits of group movement:

1   **Mirroring movements of others:** Trauma survivors get locked into survival patterns including restricted movements. By following other's movements, there is an expansion of regular movement patterns, which can stimulate new possibilities as well as open the flow of protected feelings or memories. Movement mirroring is also a feature of safe attachment for early childhood and can help a group form healthy attachments in a safe and subtle way. Finally, many people have been uncomfortable or unsafe during group movement activities (dances, family patterns, grade school or high school PE classes or sports) and this exercise can be a chance to create a safe place for corrective group movement experiences.

2   **Creating one's own movements:** Many trauma survivors have body shame or social anxiety, or self-consciousness about being seen. While this exercise can be stressful, the willingness of others to mirror and join in one's movements can be a healing experience. Over time, with increased trust and safety, individual participants can experiment (in a safe and group supported way) with new forms of movement and expression. This natural expansion helps to open soft tissue, postural and energetic pathways that are holding trauma response patterns. Finally, in a playful way, each participant has the opportunity to be consciously embodied. This experience can lead to a deeper knowledge of the intolerable/uncomfortable places inside and pleasant or alive feelings inside. All these sensations and awareness can provide a starting place for more somatic/experiential work and/or more anchored resources to facilitate the work more safely.

3   **For the practitioner:** This exercise can help the practitioner have clearer insight about each of the client's ability to be seen, their relative

comfort in their own body, and their ability to attach to the others in a group through following and leading. Also, by carefully watching movement patterns and deeply listening to clients sharing, the practitioner is alerted to places in the body that might be holding important memories or defenses, enabling the practitioner to be more effective in the clients continuing work.

DBT Skill: Alternative Rebellion

Many addicts believe if they give up their addiction they will be BORING because they've used alcohol or drugs to build up their courage in social situations. When they become sober and no longer rely on alcohol or drugs for courage, they have to become vulnerable enough to let other people see the real person inside. Instead of rebelling by abusing alcohol and drugs, use this skill, alternative rebellion, to find some other rebellious action that only you know you're doing.

For example:

- Shave your head
- Develop healthy secret thoughts
- Don't bathe every day
- Wear your underwear backwards or inside out
- Dress up or down depending on your mood
- Get a tattoo

Ask group members to self-select into smaller groups of three or four and discuss what they could do to rebel in a healthy way. Have them discuss rebellion in general and how it fits in with addiction and trauma in their lives. What is their motivation for rebellion and what benefit do they get from rebelling?

Closing: Shaking and Trembling

This exercise has three main benefits:

1. Group members have the opportunity to free up chronically held tension patterns and learn to feel their bodies (often building positive body-aware experiences).
2. Shaking and trembling are normal and necessary techniques our human being utilizes to "shake off" or "disperse" the lingering embodied stress of disregulation (fight, flight, or freeze).
3. Both the body movements and the facial expressions, done in a safe group setting, can deepen the attachment and trust within the group, restoring the joyous human qualities of play, laughter, and spontaneity that many trauma survivors have lost.

Exercise

All group members are once again in a circle, arm's length apart, if space permits.

Practitioner guides group in body movements. The suggestion, repeated throughout the exercise, is to "let the body lead":

> First one hand shaking, trembling, vibrating or moving in any way it wants.
> Then let the elbow join in so both the hand and the elbow are moving.
> Then let the shoulder join in.
> Then pause and feel the difference between the two arms. (It is very common for group members to feel pleasantly "more alive," "longer," "awakened," or "tingly.")
> Then repeat each step on the other arm.
> Pause to feel both sides of the body.
> Then each group member moves to put one hand on the wall for balance.
> The same process is gone through for the foot/knee/hip. Pausing between legs to feel the difference between both legs when standing after moving the first leg.

Then the circle comes back together, and the group is encouraged to make exaggerated facial expressions (I usually reference "Bill the Cat" or "Lucille Ball") while looking at one another. Laughter is permitted and encouraged.

30 What About My Career?

Warm Up: A Comparison Between Perfectionism and Excellence

Perfectionism

- Is Idealistic
- Says I must
- Makes Demands
- Fears Failure (insures failure)
- Focuses on Product
- Enslaves You
- Non-Accepting
- Functions in Myths

Excellence

- Is Realistic
- Says I Want
- Makes Requests
- Desires Success
- Focuses on Process
- Frees You to pursue Excellence
- Is Self-Accepting
- Functions in Reality

The above signs (found in Appendix Eight) can be laid on the floor and clients stand on the characteristics of perfectionism that has strangled their careers and brought anxiety and people pleasing. Open this discussion to the group and discuss the results. Ask: "What does excellence mean to you?"

Your Career

Your career, like life itself, is full of choices. What you choose ultimately determines success or the opportunity for improvement depending on your attitude. Until you can internalize that a bad decision is merely another learning experience, not a failure, you will forever second guess yourself and begin to turn to others for every morsel of advice, when maybe you can trust your own intuition.

Julia Cameron, author of *The Artist's Way* says: "The desire to block the fierce flow of creative energy is an underlying reason for addiction . . . We are often working to avoid ourselves, our spouses or our real feelings. We block creativity when we procrastinate, when we try to be perfect and when we fear success or failure."

Cherish your appreciation of what you *do* have instead of what you *want to have*. Set boundaries around work and have a buddy hold you accountable. Remember, failure is only absolute when you give up. Everyone gets knocked down; the question for you is will you get up? Give yourself permission to succeed. Destroy the tapes in your head telling you: "You're not good enough, smart enough or creative enough."

To experience freedom from working with others and excelling, you must work through the fear and self-doubt. Discover what your passion is and begin pursuing it. Your life's journey is to arrive at a goal you've set for yourself . . . a destination you want to reach in life. Focus on what brings you joy; what flow of expertise flows naturally from your creative juices.

According to Tolle (1999): "If these steps take up so much of your attention that they become more important than what you're doing now, you've missed your life's purpose. Your life's purpose has nothing to do with where you're going or what you're doing. It has everything to do with how you are living consciously in the present moment."

Spirituality and Intuition

What is the worst thing that can happen when you trust your own intuition? People hesitate to trust their own intuition when they're unsure of the outcome. This reflects an ultimate mistrust in a higher power. As Julia Cameron says in *The Artist's Way*: "I do the work, YOU higher power judge it." If you believed this, would it make taking the risk easier for you?

Discuss the following quotations with your group and how they relate to choosing a career.

Winston Churchill once said: "To every person there comes in their lifetime that special moment when you are figuratively tapped on the shoulder and offered the chance to do a very special thing, unique to you and your talents. What a tragedy if that moment finds you unprepared or unqualified for work that could have been your finest hour."

Rabindranath Tagore (1851–1941) wrote the following verse:

> I slept and dreamed that life was joy,
> I awoke and saw that life was duty,
> I acted and behold duty was joy.

Albert Ellis (September 27, 1913–July 24, 2007) was an American psychologist who, in 1955, developed Rational Emotive Behavior Therapy (REBT). He said: "The best years of your life are the ones in which you decide your problems are your own. You do not blame them on your mother, the ecology, or the president. You realize you control your own destiny."

Career Exercise

Split into groups of three or four.

Choose a group moderator and go around the small group and ask each person to answer the following questions:

> What is my payoff for working such long hours? Could I work less, charge more and make the same amount of money and have more time to play?
> What do I value most (family, exercise, faith, wisdom, substances, sex, gambling, etc.)?
> Am I a human being or a human doing?
> How will I feel when I finally get what I want?
> What am I going to do to get there?
> How am I spending most of my time now?
> How can I allocate differently and balance my life?
> Am I basing my own self-worth on my work? Money? What others say or think?

What will you do differently when you've discovered your passion? How will your life be different? How will you know? What will you say? Who will you include in this ideal life worth living?

DBT Skill: Pros and Cons

Pros and Cons is a DBT skill that has been used for hundreds of years to help people make better decisions. In DBT, one way we use this skill is in evaluating how we tolerate stressful situations and our reaction toward them. A person can use the skill for any decision they want to make and are having difficulty deciding. For example, an addict in treatment may be considering going to sober living or transitional living after discharge. He can use pros and cons to evaluate the advantages and disadvantages of moving back home to his normal environment or start over in a new place where he doesn't know anyone.

Pros and Cons Exercise

	Pros	Cons
Sober Living	Accountability Start Over Sober Some Freedom	Less Freedom Don't Know Anyone Curfew
Moving Back Home	Known Environment Family Support Sober Friends Support	No Accountability Old Friends Who Use Build Trust Back

Scenario/Decision

Scenario/Decision

Scenario/Decision

Closing: The End of Your Career

Have group members imagine it is the end of a long successful career and their life has come to the end. Have each person write her own eulogy, including the way she has impacted her world through her career and all of its successes.

Appendix One

Meaningful Music for Experiential Therapy

Recovery

"The Impossible Dream"	Man of La Mancha
"Wind Beneath My Wings"	Bette Midler
"Amazing Grace"	Judy Collins
"Love Can Build A Bridge"	The Judds
"Imagine"	John Lennon
"Shower the People"	James Taylor
"The River"	Garth Brooks
"All by Myself"	Eric Carmen
"I Want to Live"	John Denver
"You've Got a Friend"	Carole King
"This is My Fight Song"	Reema Roy

Death, Grief, and Loss

"Tears In Heaven"	Eric Clapton
"I'll Be There"	Escape Club
"Goodbye My Friend"	Linda Ronstadt
"Ain't No Sunshine"	Bobby Bland
"All by Myself"	Celine Dion
"Only Time"	Enya
"How Do I Live Without You?"	Andrea Alonso
"I Will Always Love You"	Whitney Houston

Healthy Relationships

"What a Wonderful World"	Louis Armstrong
"Bridge Over Troubled Water"	Simon and Garfunkel
"I Walk the Line"	Johnny Cash
"Wild Horses"	The Rolling Stones
"I Stand By You"	The Pretenders
"I Will Be Here For You"	Michael W. Smith

Disease

"Born To Be Wild"   Steppenwolf
"For Loving Me"   Gordon Lightfoot
"Desperado"   The Eagles
"Gonna Hire A Wino"   David Frizzell
"Let's Go Get Stoned"   Ray Charles
"Sober"   Pink
"Choices"   George Jones
"Wine Into Water"   T. Graham Brown
"Need You Tonight"   INXS
"Things Will Be Different"   Tracy Byrd

Spirituality

"Always Tomorrow"   Gloria Estefan
"Bridge Over Troubled Water"   Simon and Garfunkel
"Full of Grace"   Sean Johnson
"Change In My Life"   Mark Sherman
"Something To Believe In"   Poison
"We Will Find a Way"   Santana
"You Raise Me Up"   Josh Groban

Hope for the Future

"Angel"   Sarah McGlaughlin
"Bright Side of the Road"   Van Morrison
"No More Looking Over
My Shoulder"   Travis Tritt
"There's Place For Us"   Carrie Underwood
"When Love Rules the World"   Simone Angel

Inner Child

"And I Love You So"   Elvis Presley
"Beautiful Boy"   John Lennon
"Blackbird"   The Beatles
"Daddy's Little Girl"   Robin Horlock
"Gentle With Myself"   Karen Drucker
"I'll Stand By You"   The Pretenders
"Mother You"   John Lennon
"You Are So Beautiful"   Joe Cocker
"You Can Relax Now"   Shaina Noll

Parent Issues

"Because of You"	Reba McEntire
"Why?"	Jason Paige

Codependency

"Break in the Cup"	David Wilcox
"She Can't Save Him"	Reba McEntire
"In My Daughter's Eyes"	Martina McBride

Despair

"Angel"	Sarah McGlughlin
"Every Day"	Toby Lightman
"Time Machine"	Ingrid Michaelson
"Grey Room"	Damien Rice

Problems

"Hit the Road, Jack"	Ray Charles
"Like a Rock"	Paul Simon
"Money, Money, Money"	Abba
"Take a Chance on Me"	Abba
"Turn the Page"	Metallica
"Jealous"	Labrinth

Surrender

"Georgia on My Mind "	Ray Charles
"I Will Always Love You"	Whitney Houston
"End of Innocence"	Don Henley
"Water is Wide"	James Taylor
"Wasted Time"	The Eagles

Miscellaneous

"You've Got a Friend"	James Taylor
"I Can't Make You Love Me"	Bonnie Raitt
"And So it Goes"	Billy Joel
"Angry Young Man"	Billy Joel
"I Need You"	Celine Dion
"Live Like You Were Dying"	Tim McGraw
"Let It Be"	The Beatles
"Purple Rain"	Prince
"Somebody Love Me"	Ella Fitzgerald
"I'm Alive"	Neil Diamond
"Song Sung Blue"	Neil Diamond

Numbness

Yearning

and

Searching

Disorganization

Anger

Despair

Reorganization

Reinvestment

ADDICTIVE BEHAVIORS

CYNICISM/ SARCASM

PASSIVE AGGRESSIVE BEHAVIOR

RAGE

DEPRESSION

IF I FORGIVE IT MEANS I APPROVE OF WHAT WAS DONE TO ME

I CAN NEVER FORGIVE MYSELF

EVEN IF I FORGIVE I WILL NEVER FORGET

IF I FORGIVE, IT MEANS I WANT TO HAVE A RELATIONSHIP WITH THE PERSON I'M FORGIVING

IF I FORGIVE, I WILL NO LONGER BE ANGRY AT THE PERSON FOR WHAT HAPPENED

IF I FORGIVE, MY RELATIONSHIP WITH THE PERSON I'M FORGIVING WILL IMPROVE

IF I FORGIVE MYSELF I'LL MORE LIKELY DO IT AGAIN

IF I HAVEN'T FORGOTTEN IT MEANS I HAVEN'T REALLY FORGIVEN

I FORGIVE FOR THE SAKE OF THE OTHER PERSON

PERFECTIONISM

RELAPSE

DISTRACTIONS

PROCRASTINATION

UNHEALTHY EATING

LACK OF EXERCISE

LACK OF SKILLS

Emotions

Work

Self-Care

Relationships

Spirituality

Other

Appendix Seven
Irrational Beliefs Sociometry Cards

**There is a right way to feel
in every situation
Letting others know that I am
feeling bad is a weakness
Negative feelings are bad
and destructive
Being emotional means being out
of control
Emotions can just happen for
no reason
Some emotions are really stupid
All painful emotions are a result
of a bad attitude
If others don't approve of my
feelings, I obviously
shouldn't feel the way I do
Other people are the best judge of
how I am feeling
Painful emotions are not really
important and should be ignored**

Perfectionism Is Idealistic

Perfectionism Says I must

Perfectionism Makes Demands

Perfectionism Fears Failure (insures failure)

Perfectionism Focuses on Product

Perfectionism Enslaves you

Perfectionism Non-Accepting

Perfectionism Functions in Myths

Excellence Is Realistic

Excellence
Says I Want

Excellence Makes
Requests

Excellence
Desires Success

Excellence Focuses on Process

Excellence Frees You to Pursue Excellence

Excellence Is Self-Accepting

Excellence Functions in Reality

References

Bandler, R. (1985). *Using your brain – for a change*, Moab, UT, Real People Press.

Cameron, J. (1992). *The artist's way: A spiritual path to higher creativity*, New York, TarcherPerigee.

Carnes, P. (1997). *The betrayal bond: Breaking free of exploitive relationships*, Deerfield Beach, FL, HCI Books.

Dayton, T. (2011). *Relationship trauma repair: An experiential multi-sensory process for healing PTSD*, Deerfield Beach, FL, Unrivaled Books.

Flores, P. (2004). *Addiction as an attachment disorder*, New York, Jason Aronson, Inc.

Koerner, K. (2012). *Doing dialectical behavior therapy: A practical guide*, New York, Guilford Press.

Linehan, M.M. (1993). *Cognitive-behavioral treatment for borderline personality disorder*, New York, Guilford Press.

Linehan, M.M. (1993). *Skills training manual for treating borderline personality disorder*, New York, Guilford Press.

Linehan, M.M. (2015). *DBT skills training handouts and worksheets*, second edition, New York, Guilford Press.

McKay, M., Wood, J.C., & Brantley, J. (2007). *The dialectical behavior therapy skills workbook: Practical DBT exercises for learning mindfulness, interpersonal effectiveness, emotion regulation & distress tolerance*, Oakland, CA, New Harbinger Publications.

Marston, M.M. (2002). *Emotions of normal people*, Abingdon, Routledge.

Mellody, P., & Miller, A.W. (1989). *Breaking free: A recovery workbook for facing codependence*, San Francisco, CA, HarperCollins Publishers.

Potter-Efron, R., & Potter-Efron, P. (1989). *Letting go of shame: Understanding how shame affects your life*, Center City, MN, Hazeldon Publishing.

Schutzenberger, A.A. (1966). *Précis de psychodrame*, Paris, Editions Universitaires.

Sikes, R. (1990). Why affirmations don't work and how you can replace them with directed questions™ to get the results you want, http://idea-seminars.com/articles/affirm.htm.

Tolle, E. (1999). *The power of now*, Novato, CA, New World Library.

Wegscheider-Cruse, S., Cruse, J.R., & Bougher, G. (1990). *Experiential therapy for co-dependency*, Palo Alto, CA, Science and Behavior Books, Inc.

Wegscheider-Cruse, S., Higby, K., Klontz, T., & Rainey, A. (1994). *Family reconstruction: The living theater model*, Palo Alto, CA, Science and Behavior Books, Inc.

Woodmansee, S.M. (2011). *Dialectical behavior therapy experiential exercises*, Denver, CO, Self.

Index